Made to Thrive

Eight Courageous Practices to Improve Your Life, Find Inner Peace and Be Happy

Denise Garrett

ISBN: 978-0-9990437-0-7 (paperback)
Library of Congress Control Number: 2017914901

Cover design by Nathan Dasco

Printed in USA by Denise Garrett

The publisher has strived to be as accurate and complete as possible in the creation of this book. The author's intent is to provide information to help you in your quest for spiritual, emotional and physical well-being. In practical advice books, as in anything else in life, there are no guarantees of results. The advice and strategies found within may not be suitable for every situation. This work is sold with the understanding that neither the author nor the publisher are held responsible for the results accrued from the advice in this book. The author of this book does not dispense medical advice or prescribe the use of any technique, either directly or indirectly, as a form of treatment for medical, physical or emotional problems, without consulting a competent healthcare professional.

While all attempts have been made to verify information provided for this publication, the publisher assumes no responsibility for errors, omissions, or contrary interpretation of the subject matter herein. Any perceived slights of specific persons, peoples, or organizations are unintended.

For more information, visit www.denisegarrett.com

For bulk book orders, contact Denise Garrett via email: denise@denisegarrett.com

Table of Contents

Dedication

This book is dedicated to the love of my life and to my fellow fire-fighter brothers and sisters, the brave men and women who place themselves in harm's way to protect and serve others.

Acknowledgments

Lisa, the love of my life, who inspires me to be my best and who makes my life so much better by simply being you.

Mom, my greatest teacher, in making love a verb. Without her love and generosity, I would not be who I am today.

Dad, for instilling your spirit of adventure in me, and for embracing your gay daughter without making me feel bad and wrong.

Mike, my coach, who loved me enough to be ruthlessly honest with me and for courageously calling me on my stuff. My coach, Rob, who gave me the courage to be my authentic self and who taught me the power of a vision.

To my teachers, especially David and Wanda Gail. David for teaching me to throw away the notes and give people me. Wanda Gail for demonstrating how to balance the spontaneous draw of one's heart with the practical actions needed to get things done. Chuck Johnson for showing up when I needed you most at the hospital that day and for asking me the one question that has fueled my courage to follow my dreams.

Diana, my book shepherd, without whom I would not have made it into print thereby realizing one of my big dreams.

Clare, for the courageous feedback you provided that helped me find my voice, and for the endless hours you devoted to helping me perfect my message.

Donna, Cindy, Tracie, Lisa D., Lindsey, Emmaki, Kit and Lisa P. for supporting me in getting my message onto a bigger platform. Your time and input made for a better book and stronger message.

To First Responders (e.g., Police, Fire, Paramedics, Emergency Medical Technicians, and Sheriffs) who are brave enough to show up for people when they are having their worst day. You continue to inspire and amaze me.

Preface

I'm five years old and hiding in the closet of my bedroom.

I squeeze my favorite stuffed animal, Poochie, close to me; he indulgently absorbs my tears.

I am waiting for it stop.

I beg and plead with a God I've never seen to make it better.

My parents are fighting again.

I hear their clamoring angry voices yelling vicious words. Their insults are so venomous and toxic they singe the air.

With each word missile launched, I sense the fabric of my parents' happiness ripping apart.

Afterwards, their bloody soul wounds ooze misery, hurt, anger, disappointment and frustration.

Sadness consumes our home and completely engulfs me.

I want out, but there's nowhere to go. I don't want to be here. "Make it stop, please, God!" I silently pray.

Physical blows are never exchanged. They are not needed, for the violent potency of their words inflict enough damage.

They attack each other's personhood, going right to the essence of one another's being.

Something in me knows it does not have to be like this. I know there is a better way to live and to love.

After each battle in their war with words, they seek comfort from me.

"Why is your mama this way? Why can't she be more like that?"

"Why is your dad such a mean bully? Why can't he be more thoughtful and considerate?"

I am deeply affected by the way they assault each other with words.

The unspoken question I hear is, "Why can't you make it better, Denise?"

I try as hard as I know how, but nothing I do works.

Maybe if I'm a good girl, they won't argue so much.

Even though I am as kind and sweet as I know how to be, my attempts to heal their pain are too meager to make a difference.

I beg them to stop when they argue, but my pleas fall on deaf ears.

I provide what little comfort any five-year-old child can provide, but it's not enough to stop their fighting or to make them happy.

All I want is for my parents to be happy, and they aren't. It must be my fault.

To cope with the overwhelming heartbreak, I retreat inside myself.

Solitude is my respite. God is my saving grace.

Stubbornness keeps me afloat in the sea of heartache that I call home until I can get out and pursue my own happiness.

My daddy often says, "You've got a triple dose of stubborn in you, Denise Garrett!" According to him, I inherited his stubbornness, my mama's stubbornness, and came into the world with my own special brand of it.

Dad shares how he watches me after telling me not to do something. If a certain look comes across my face, he knows I am going to do it anyway.

On one occasion, after doing what he told me not to do, I come back to him and bend over, exclaiming, "I'm ready for my spanking, Daddy!"

~*~

It seems I have a keen awareness that we face consequences for the choices we make.

Sadly, many of the choices we make are unconscious.

The one thing I wanted most as a little girl was for my parents to stop fighting, to be happy and love each other.

When I could not make this happen, I unconsciously decided that I was a worthless failure.

This led to an unconscious belief that the world would be a better place without me in it, which made my life a living hell for years.

At a young age, I made a conscious commitment to myself that I would never fight the way my parents fought.

Flash forward many years to my first serious long-term relationship. When we would have a disagreement, I would automatically become withdrawn.

Distancing myself helped me avoid fighting like my parents fought, but it did not help solve the issues and challenges my partner and I faced, nor did it diminish my pain.

Flash forward again to the tragedies I responded to as a firefighter where I gained an appreciation for the expression that war is hell. *Home can be hell too, but it's our minds that take us there and back.*

Thankfully, I had three big things working in my favor:

1. An extra-sensory awareness of a Loving Presence always with me
2. My unwavering belief that there had to be a better way to live and to love
3. My stubborn determination to pursue a better life

By stubbornly pursing a better way to live and to love, I discovered the eight courageous practices in this book.

These eight practices have significantly improved the quality of my life and relationships. They have also given me a profound sense of inner peace and happiness.

Before I discovered the eight courageous practices, I felt like life was a game of survival. After engaging in these practices, I'm convinced that I, and everyone else, is made to thrive.

To me, thriving means that:

- I feel better about myself (i.e., who I am and how I interact with others).
- I am optimistic about my opportunities and possibilities.
- I get better results – in relationships, at work and at play.

I believe you were made to thrive.

No matter how great or bad things seem in your life right now, I believe things can get better.

I want you to feel good about yourself, to feel optimistic about your future and to get results that satisfy your soul.

By implementing these eight courageous practices in your life, I believe you will shift from merely surviving to positively thriving!

Stuff 101

The Stuff that Causes Pain

Question: If I offered you $100,000 to jump out of an airplane without a parachute, would you do it?

I bet you said no!

But what if I told you the airplane was on the ground?

Did your answer change once you knew the airplane was on the ground?

Did you notice your automatic, knee-jerk answer to the first question?

Many people change their answer from "no" to "yes" once they learn that the airplane is on the ground. What caused their answer to change? Receiving better information which went beyond their initial automatic knee-jerk reaction.

What caused them to say no in the first place?

Fear.

As the first female firefighter in Gwinnett County, Georgia, I know something about fear and what it takes to triumph over it. I'm often asked if it was scary running into burning buildings. The honest answer is: yes, it was—but I did what firefighters do.

I did not let gnawing fear stop me.

As scary as running into a burning building is, each day we face something that is far less scary, but is just as deadly.

Most of the time when we encounter this toxic invisible substance, we aren't aware of it.

This substance is the root cause of our pain. It sucks the life force out of us, stealing our joy and causing our dreams to die. This lethal substance is so pervasive it has contaminated our planet. It's the deadliest force known to you, me, and humankind.

This fatal invisible force is our fear.

Fear is easy to recognize and respond to when the external challenge we face is big and noticeable, like a burning building. It's easy to see how the fear of a tornado, wildfire, or tsunami gets in our way.

It's *much* harder to detect the lethal toll fear takes on us when the danger we face is internal and subtle. It's difficult to defeat an invisible enemy, but it's not impossible.

Fear is the stuff that causes our pain and misery. This book shows you how to identify the subtle and not-so-subtle fears that suck the life force out of you. At the same time, it offers eight practices for developing and strengthening your courage muscles, equipping you to manage your fear.

As you become more adept at managing your fear, you will feel better and get better results in your life.

What Gets in Your Way?

When asked what caused my pain, I had automatic, knee-jerk responses to the question. My responses included things like:

- Certain childhood events.
- Lack of money.
- Not enough time.
- Certain obstinate, hateful people.
- Lacking the right connections.
- Not having the skills or talent to do something I wanted to do.

If you are like me, you can generate a list of what you think causes your pain. Give it a try. On a piece of paper, write the first things that come to mind.

What's in your way?

Notice the word fear does not appear in my list, and it may not appear in your list, either. That's how subtle fear can be. Fear wears disguises, yet it's fear that gets in our way. Fear is universal, mucky stuff that starts inside of each one of us by grabbing us in its powerful clutches through our thoughts.

Fear causes my pain while stealing my joy. To show this, here are a few examples of how fear shows up in my life:

- I worry about not being good enough.
- I'm concerned that others might view me as worthless.
- At times, I feel useless.
- I have flaws and imperfections.
- I don't get some things right.
- I make mistakes.
- I miss things.
- I screw up.
- Sometimes I don't achieve what I set out to achieve.

I bring this stuff, or fear, into my relationships with others. As good as I am, my concerns about these issues creep into most aspects of my life.

My fearful thoughts affect my:

- Career path.
- Finances and material wealth.
- Family.
- Relationships.

- Health.
- Spirituality and/or religion.
- Peace of mind.
- Happiness and joy.
- Discoveries.
- Possibilities.

You may worry about different matters. Your concerns may show up differently in your life. Make no mistake; your life is riddled with fear too. You might have concerns about not being smart enough or worries about being seen as a loser.

You might be afraid that you are unlovable. You might have issues around entitlement or stuff about being arrogant. You may struggle over a multitude of qualities that might be perceived as negative because you worry about what people think about you.

Getting a handle on this stuff and how to move beyond it is the goal of this book. It looks at how fear impacts your pain, and then teaches you eight courageous practices to feel better and get better results in your life.

To get the most out of this book, I recommend you follow the tips provided below.

Getting Started – How to Get the Most Out of This Endeavor

Right now, you may be thinking: Denise, you don't know me. You don't know what I'm going through.

You may push back against my proposed solutions because it's not a one-size-fits-all kind of world.

You are correct to think this.

I'm not saying that my answers are the same as your answers, nor am I suggesting that what works for me will work for you. At the same time, I want you to get the most out of this endeavor, and if you heed the following tips, it's possible.

Tip #1 – Try It On

Treat the contents of this book as if you were shopping for a coat on the rack at your favorite store. Try each concept on to see how well it fits you before ignoring or discarding it.

If it works for you and fits, great! Keep it.

If it doesn't work for you, no worries. Place it back on the rack and keep shopping. There are plenty of coats—or tools—for you to choose from! The most important thing is to choose what works for you.

Tip #2 – Answer Questions for Yourself

This book contains several key questions. To get the most out of this venture, *answer the questions for yourself.* These questions are for you. Be honest with yourself, and don't judge your answers.

Just answer. There is no right or wrong answer, only the one that you make, which is the most important one.

This book is about you discovering how to feel better and get better results.

Tip #3 – Resistance Means Something Has Its Hooks in You

While there is no one right way to engage with the material contained in this book, pay attention to anything you resist.

Remember: what we resist, persists.

I discovered that the more I resist, the bigger the cosmic two-by-fours the universe whoops me with. This goes on until I finally relent and listen to whatever it is the universe wants me to attend to.

Do yourself a favor: adopt an attitude that when you find yourself resisting something, something has its hooks in you. You won't be free until you unhook.

Stay with it.

Tip #4 – You Are Golden

Tip four comes with the story of the Golden Buddha, and the first big clue on how to break free from our "stuff":

> *Imagine that you are worth millions of dollars, but your worth is concealed by a protective layer of armor. One day, you are injured. A crack appears in your armor, revealing your true worth. With your protective layer removed, people know you are worth millions.*

> *The Temple of the Golden Buddha at Wat Traimit near Chinatown in Bangkok is home to the world's largest seated gold statue of Buddha. Shrouded in a cloud of mystery, historians speculate that the huge statue was concealed in clay to protect it from looters and invading armies. The statue was disguised so well that people forgot what was hidden beneath. The heavy statue dropped as it was hoisted into its new home at Wat Traimit. A crack appeared in the clay revealing the gold underneath.*

The way I see it, we are *all* Golden Buddhas, and we are all sacred.

Sometimes, we get glimpses of our sacredness and magnificence when we are in action. Other times, our greatness frightens us or the people around us, so we cover it up.

When we are lucky, we meet people (parents, friends, lovers, spouses, coaches, teachers, mentors) who shine a light on our brilliance, extending us an invitation to fully express it.

We are shrouded in the muck and mire of fear, which keeps us from realizing our dreams. By examining this fear and distinguishing between what works for us and what doesn't, we gain access to what we need to do so we can feel better and get better results in our lives.

To get the most out of this book, adopt the point of view that there is something important to examine when it causes you to:

- Be upset.
- Get your hackles up.
- Have your feathers ruffled.
- Feel the need to defend yourself, your position, or your choices.
- Feel anger, hurt, sadness, or disappointment.
- Feel like a victim, a persecutor, or the need to rescue.
- Have strong judgments of right/wrong or good/bad.
- Insist that you are right and the other person is wrong.
- Feel any other feeling that takes away your joy and your sense of peace.

I've discovered that reactions like the ones listed above act as shards of clay that muck up the light and power inside me. These are indicators that I have work to do. These fear-based reactions show that it's time for me to use one of the tools contained in this book so that I can knock off yet another shard of clay.

The more I use the tools contained in this book, the more powerful and influential I become. The more I practice, the better I feel, and the more effective I become. As you implement these tools, you will also begin to feel better and get better results in your life too.

The Two Main Pain Producers

Fear comes in many cunning disguises. The following stories illustrate two crucial points about fear. Failure to understand these points will result in you staying stuck in your stuff.

The first point is that fear is automatic. The second point is that fear makes me right, which makes me blind.

As you read the first story, try to notice where your thoughts tend to go.

Farmer Story

There was a farmer who had one horse.

One day, his horse ran away.

The neighbors came to console him over his terrible loss.

The farmer said, "What makes you think it is so terrible?"

A month later, the horse came home bringing two beautiful wild horses with her.

The neighbors were excited about the farmer's good fortune. "Such lovely strong horses! What good fortune your mare has brought you!" they professed.

"What makes you think this is good fortune?" the farmer asked.

Several days later, the farmer's son was thrown from one of the wild horses and broke his leg.

The neighbors cried out in distress, "Such bad luck!"

The farmer asked, "What makes you think this is bad?"

A war came to the area and every able-bodied man was conscripted into battle.

The farmer's son was not because of his broken leg.

The neighbors congratulated the farmer on his good luck.

"What makes you think this is good?" the farmer asked.

Did you notice how easy it is to judge situations as good or bad, and how fast we do this?

First crucial point: fear automatically causes me to judge situations and people as good or bad, and I do this in the blink of an eye.

Have you ever done something you are embarrassed about?

I have!

In this next tale, I'm going to tell a personal story which illustrates the second crucial point. You will need to understand this to free yourself from fear that gets in your way: *being right makes me blind.*

The Broken Air Conditioner(AC):Also Known as Being Right Makes Me Blind

Years ago, I flipped on the AC in my car and discovered that it was not working.

It was a very hot day.

I was on my way to a meeting and wanted to look my best for it.

I immediately became frustrated at the unfairness of my situation.

The further I drove, the hotter and more upset I became.

In a fit of anger, I slammed my fist on the dashboard of my car.

That's when I noticed that the vents on my dashboard were closed.

The AC was working fine.

As fast as flipping a switch, I automatically assumed that my AC wasn't working.

Had anyone challenged me about the AC not working, I would have been adamant that it was broken.

I was right! My AC was not working!

That is... until I noticed that the vents were closed.

Being right about the AC not working caused me to *stop* looking for other solutions and possibilities. That's why it is vital that you understand the second crucial point:

When you insist that you are right about something or someone, you stop looking for other solutions and possibilities.

Notice how we automatically judge situations as good or bad, and we think we are right about them.

The average person has 50,000 – 70,000 thoughts each day. This means that we judge ourselves, people and situations an average of 60,000 times each day. We believe that our judgments are right, which means we may kill off 60,000 greater possibilities each day. These are possibilities that have an infinite capacity to make us feel better and produce better results.

The Vampires that Rob Our Power and Cause Tremendous Pain: Drama and Upsets

Drama

Now, let me bring your attention to a story that runs rampant in our culture, often causing the most pain and strife in our lives. It's a story we are addicted to as surely as a heroin addict is addicted to heroin.

I call this story drama.

Drama involves terrible situations and consists of a dance between three main characters: Victim, Rescuer, Persecutor. Without these three main characters, drama does not exist. A typical drama story is filled with people making other people and events bad and wrong.

It's dramatic when a house catches on fire. The occupants of the house become victims of the terrible, persecutory fire until the firefighter rescuers rush in to save the day. This scenario involves actual danger. We do not face this kind of danger very often.

An Important Distinction | A Distinction that May Save Your Life

This gives rise to an important distinction. The distinction between danger, threats, and fear. This book focuses on *perceived* threats, not danger. Danger is a person, place or thing (e.g., fire, cliff, toxin, weapon), with the capacity and/or intent to cause me immediate physical or emotional harm.

A threat is an assessment of harm that *may* or *may not* happen and-fear is a mental reaction to that perceived threat. Most of the threats we perceive do not result in us being physically harmed. In many instances, fear is a mental trick I play on myself or allow someone else to play on me.

When my house is on fire, I am in a dangerous and threatening situation. I may perceive someone judging me as a threat, but I am not in danger. It's easy to allow our minds to trick us into perceiving we are in peril when there is no danger. Think back to the Farmer Story, and how fast the neighbors judged the situations as good or bad.

Right/wrong, good/bad conversations are sparked when we perceive a person or situation to be a threat. When events happen in our lives, thoughts surge automatically through our consciousness, and these thoughts are usually based on some determination of right/wrong, good/bad, or agree/disagree.

It's as if we are constantly scanning for the threat. No wonder our stories are filled with so much pain! These right/wrong, good/bad conversations produce drama because they box people into the roles of victim, persecutor, or rescuer.

When I feel persecuted, I feel threatened.

When I feel persecuted, I assume the role of victim and am looking for someone to rescue me.

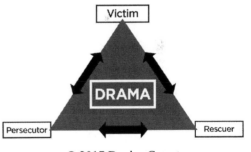

© 2017 Denise Garret

I assume the role of rescuer when someone is hurt and I rush to their aid.

I become the persecutor when (a) I intentionally hurt someone, or (b) someone tells me that I hurt their feelings or harmed them in some way.

It's not uncommon to shift from role to role on the drama triangle. I may start out as a rescuer, only to be told that I did the wrong thing, which then causes me to feel persecuted.

When I feel persecuted, I feel like a victim. The drama dance has been going on for centuries as evidenced by historic events, movies, music, television, and the stories we pass down from generation to generation.

The problem with drama is that to have drama, somebody must get hurt. When I'm caught up in drama, I lose sight of my true nature; that I, like most people, am powerful beyond measure.

Even though drama requires someone to be wounded, it seems as if the drama dance is embedded in my DNA because it's so comfortable and familiar. Thankfully, years ago I discovered a way to get off the drama triangle, and now I know how to stop buying tickets to that sad, old dance.

To get free from the pain of drama, I need to do one simple thing: stop blaming anyone, including myself, for anything.

I blame others so I can avoid taking responsibility for and being accountable for my own actions. Blame gets me a lot of attention. Blame makes other people feel sorry for me. Blame places the responsibility out there somewhere.

However, when the responsibility, or the ability to respond, lies outside of me, I have given my power away. I cannot create what I want to create when I am busy blaming.

The most surefire way to get what I want in life is to take personal responsibility for it. When I take responsibility for achieving or obtaining something, I become a magnet for that thing.

I attract to me the things that aid in the manifestation of it. Case in point: how I became a firefighter.

When I graduated from college, I complied with what my parents and other elders told me I needed to do to succeed:

I went to work in corporate America. I was fortunate to obtain a good position with a reputable company, and I was living the American dream.

I did well in my new position, getting promoted within six months to an even better position. But there was one big problem: I was miserable. The corporate environment at the company I worked for was stifling my spirit, so I began searching for other options.

I wanted to do work that satisfied my soul, so I started paying attention to activities that brought me joy and gave me a greater sense of fulfillment. While I did not know exactly where I wanted to go, I committed myself to finding work that fed my soul.

At the time, I played soccer. My team would hang out at a local pub after games. It was here that I met someone who would play a pivotal role in my career path.

Sitting around the table at the pub one day, I met a woman who was friends with one of my teammates. She struck up a conversation with me. We had a lot in common. We both liked science. We both loved exercising. We also enjoyed dismantling and building things with our own two hands.

She mentioned that she'd heard I was looking to make a career change which I confirmed. She asked me, "Have you ever thought about being a firefighter?"

What?

I told her, "Women don't do that!" to which she responded, "Actually, they do. I'm a woman, and I'm a firefighter." My next response was, "But you can die doing that!" At that time, I was not open to exploring firefighting as a career option. Despite my initial rejection, she had successfully planted a seed that day, and that seed took root.

I asked her lots of questions about what firefighters do. The more I learned, the more the job spoke to me. I loved the idea of using science and my physical, mental, and spiritual prowess to serve others. This became a burning desire for me.

Several weeks later, I called her up and asked what one needed to do to become a firefighter. She told me about the hiring process which involved a written exam, a background check, a drug test, a psychological evaluation, a physical agility test, and a formal panel interview by the Fire Chief and several Battalion Chiefs. At this point, I was committed to becoming a firefighter. I did not know when or where I would get hired as a firefighter, I just knew I was going to be a firefighter—no matter what.

That's when the magic happened. I came across a book that helped me prepare for the written exam. While I had been working out avidly, I knew I needed to up my game to pass the physical agility test. A wonderful guy at my gym volunteered to help me push beyond the training plateaus I hit along the way. Another person volunteered to help me practice for the formal interview. Magically, the stars aligned so that I got time off from work to take each test required. My commitment, training, and hard work paid off. The county I most wanted to work for offered me the job. I accepted the position with one major surprise. I was that county's first female firefighter.

The moment I decided to pursue work that I enjoyed, possibilities opened that would otherwise have remained hidden to me. The moment I formed a new belief that women could be firefighters, I gained access to a path toward greater happiness that had previously been hidden.

The moment I decided to become a firefighter and take responsibility for doing the things I knew I needed to do, magic happened. This would not have happened if I'd stayed in the stifling corporate environment, blaming the circumstances, the company, my parents, or society for my misery.

Our fear-based beliefs keep us entrenched in drama and blame.

New beliefs usher in new experiences.

The universe and everything in it is constantly shifting. Things that did not seem possible yesterday are possible and happening today. Beliefs are malleable and transient. As rock tumblers polish stones, my polished beliefs smooth away the rough edges that keep me from my greater good. We can polish our fear-based beliefs and smooth away our pain by addressing our upsets.

How Drama and Upsets Kill Us

When I shared the story of the AC not working in my car, I shared how I got upset over something that was not even true (the belief that my AC was broken). The truth was that the AC was working, but the vents were closed, making it appear as if the AC was broken. I shared how being right about the AC not working caused me to stop looking for other solutions and possibilities.

I was scared that showing up drenched in sweat would make a bad impression. I was anxious about how much it would cost to repair my AC. This internal conversation about the broken AC triggered my body's physiological fight or flight response as it readied itself to deal with the perceived threat of the broken AC.

My heart rate increased, and my blood pressure rose. My nervous system performed activities designed to help me respond to the threats I perceived. My system flooded with special hormones designed to help me deal with the threat.

Whether the threat we perceive is real or imagined, it takes our body 20 to 60 minutes to return to its pre-arousal levels of these hormones-after the threat is removed. Repeated and/or sustained activation of the fight or flight response has been linked to many of the stress-related symptoms prevalent in our society today.

Stress-related symptoms include:

- Headaches.
- Upset stomach (e.g., diarrhea, constipation, nausea).
- Aches, pains, and muscle tension.
- Chest pain.
- Insomnia.
- Frequent illnesses.
- Easily agitated or moody.
- Constant worrying.
- Inability of focus.
- Changes in appetite (e.g., not eating, or overeating).
- Procrastinating.
- Increased use of alcohol, drugs, or tobacco products.

Fear often starts as a conversation. Conversations steeped in drama, blame, and upsets can trigger our fight or flight response. Over time, repeated and/or sustained activation of the fight or flight response may be detrimental to our health and well-being.

Fear is a mental reaction to a perceived threat that may or may not occur. Zig Ziglar said, "Fear has two meanings: forget everything and run, or face everything and rise; the choice is yours."

What would make you feel better?

- What scares you, worries you, concerns you, and causes you anxiety, fear, and doubt?
- Identify 3 to 5 things you know you have a knee-jerk, automatic reaction to, and be honest: how well is this working for you?

- In what areas of life are you experiencing the most pain or discord?
  - In your career or business?
  - In your finances?
  - In your relationships?
  - In your health?
- Are you willing to follow the tips provided in this book so that you can get the most out of this endeavor? (Hint: These tips also help us get the most out of life.)
- Observe your automatic, knee-jerk judgments. Do you see how they contribute to your pain and how they keep you from getting better results?
- Can you see how being right stops you from looking for other possibilities and opportunities that might work better for you?
- Can you see how being right might create damage in your relationships?
- Do you have drama in your life?
- Are you willing to stop running the drama story and stop playing the blame game so you can experience greater happiness and freedom?
- What are you upset about?
- Are drama and upsets affecting your health?
- Are you willing to take courageous actions to address your upsets?

It is my hope that by increasing your awareness of how fear shows up in your life and providing you with tools to manage your fear more effectively, you will feel better.

Not just that, but also to give you the gift of experiencing unprecedented levels of happiness, peace, freedom, health, and fulfillment.

A Special Bonus from Denise

Now that you have your copy of *Made to Thrive: Eight Coura-geous Practices to Improve Your Life, Find Inner Peace and Be Happy*, you are on your way to:

- Feeling better about yourself (i.e., who you are and how you interact with others)
- Feeling optimistic about your opportunities and possibilities
- Getting better results in your relationships, at work and at play

Plus...you'll soon find yourself experiencing more peace and happiness.

You'll also receive the special bonus journal I created to add to your toolkit. The journal gives you a central place to capture your responses to the questions contained inside. You may want to refer back to your answers as you grow and expand, or face different challenges moving forward.

There's so much confusing information out there about how to improve your life, find inner peace and happiness. When you finish this book, you'll be armed with eight courageous practices that will help you feel better and get better results.

While this journal is offered for sale, as a special bonus you can claim it for free here:

www.denisegarrett.com/bookbonus.

I believe you were made to thrive.

I'm in your corner. Let me know if I can help further.

Here's to you creating a life where you positively thrive!

Best,
Denise Garrett

Chapter 1

The First Courageous Practice – Identifying Where You Are

The first courageous practice calls for us to assess where we are now. When you are going on a trip, you start by mapping out your course from where you are now to where you want to go.

With maps, GPS, and various forms of transportation, most people have a pretty good handle on maneuvering from one geographical location to another. Sadly, we are not as adept at figuring out what keeps us stuck in our pain, feeling bad, and not getting better results. We don't know how to get where we want to go because we don't understand where we are now.

Imagine for a moment that life is like a giant bowl of vegetable soup. There's the broth that represents the creative medium in which we live, move, and have our being.

The soup also has big, fat carrots, diced tomatoes, chunks of celery, diced potatoes, beans, and other ingredients, each one acting as beliefs and paradigms that keep us from rising to the top where our dreams live.

As we float along in life, we bump up against the limiting beliefs and paradigms that surround us in the giant soup bowl of life.

Floating along one day, something happens. We experience a flash of insight or a moment of brilliant inspiration. A dream is born: we see beyond the upper edge of the soup bowl and imagine for a moment how things could be different.

Two seconds later, as we call our best friend or share our shiny new dream with our spouse, they throw their *soup du jour* on us.

Splat!

Their limiting belief smacks us in our most tender, vulnerable place. Because our insightful dream and inspiration is in its infancy, it's not strong enough to propel itself forward. When we buy into their fear, our embryonic dream dies as fast as it was born.

It's easy to get caught up in the soup of other people's beliefs about what is possible and what isn't possible. It's more straightforward to blame others for not supporting my dream than it is to take personal responsibility for pursuing it.

It's not difficult to buy into the paradigms people have for what it means to be a leader, to be successful, or to be masculine or feminine. It's simple because that is what I see with my eyes when I gaze out upon the world.

I see evidence that men are this way and women are that way. The media provides me with ample evidence of what society at large believes leaders look like, and what success looks like. The media shows me evidence that people believe in conflict, in war, in violence, in illness, in poverty, in scarcity, and in fear.

Fear

The first step in gaining the upper hand over fear is understanding what causes it. Fear is triggered whenever I am concerned that my needs won't be met. Fear gets triggered whenever I'm afraid that my needs for the following won't be met:

- Basic survival (e.g., physiological needs for food, shelter, clothing, sleep, oxygen).
- Safety and security (e.g., health, physical safety, employment, resources, stability).
- Love and belonging (e.g., love, acceptance, and belonging).

- Esteem (e.g., self-esteem, confidence, achievement, competence, respect, acknowledgment).
- Self-actualization (e.g., reaching my full potential).

Fear is easy to recognize when It's loud and violent, angry yelling and shaking fists. When I feel like yelling, arguing, or shaking my fists, it's easy for me to appreciate that underneath the bluster I'm *afraid.*

It's also unmistakable that I'm *scared* when I face a situation that has my heart pounding and/or my knees quivering.

Another kind of fear sneaks in through the back door of my consciousness, robbing me of choice before I realize what's happening.

I call this flavor of fear sneaky fear.

Sneaky fear wears many clever disguises and is quite the seductress. This makes it very dangerous because it leaves a wake of missed opportunities and destruction in its path.

Diagnosing Sneaky Fear

Sneaky fear is a master chameleon, and it often comes disguised as a:

- Friendly ally looking out for my best interests.
- Seemingly legitimate concern, often based on historical data or statistics.
- Concern over being left behind, left out, or not belonging.
- Worry about the supply or Source not being enough.
- Concern about being dominated, controlled, subservient, or submissive.
- Worry about losing, or the potential for loss.

It's still difficult to recognize when sneaky fear rears its ugly head inside of me, but spotting its appearance in other people has helped me become better at spotting it in myself.

Symptoms of sneaky fear include:

- Being fixated on"Ain't it awful."
- Statements like:
    - "That's the way it's always been."
    - "Things will never change."
    - "I can't."
    - "You'll never…"
    - "You're too <fill in the blank>" or "it's too <fill in the blank>, or "you are not <fill in the blank>, or you don't have <fill in the blank>."
- Positions people take when they:
    - Defend their position about why they are right about anything.
    - Insist on telling you that if you pursue that dream, <fill in the blank reason> why you will fail.
    - Feel compelled to inform you that you will fail because "according to the latest <news reports, research, trends>."

Fear Keeps Us Scanning for Threats

When I am exhibiting one of these symptoms, I understand that sneaky fear has got its hooks in me. I can also detect sneaky fear by paying attention to what I'm scanning for in the conversations I have with others. It's as if I have a default setting that tunes my ears to pick up potential threats. The threats I'm scanning for include concerns I have about:

- How other people see me.
- My past failures.
- My time.

Most of us want to make a good impression on other people. After all, people won't hire us or keep us around if they don't like us. When

I'm worried about how other people see me, I scan conversations for clues about how they see me. Since I want to make sure I look good, I worry about saying something that will impress them, or that will make them like me.

As I'm listening to them, I scan for things that I may have in common with them, for how we are similar, and for whether they agree with me. In extreme cases, if I am afraid you'll think I am stupid, I won't even hear you. I'm too busy showing you how I already know more than you know; I've already heard it, done it, and said it better than you.

The problem with worrying about looking good is that sometimes I need to share something that you need to hear—but might not like hearing it—so I don't.

The same goes for you. You may have something to tell me that would improve the quality of my life but won't tell me because you are worried about looking good.

The most prominent way our fear about looking good shows up is that we are compulsive judging and voting machines. We want to look good. It's as if our physical and emotional well-being depends on us looking good.

The predominant way we reduce our fear about looking good lies in how we automatically judge what is good and what is bad, what is right, and what is wrong, what we agree with, and what we disagree with.

The problem with us being judging and voting machines is that once we decide we are right, we kill off other possibilities, many of which might be better for all concerned.

When I'm worried about my past failures, I tend to scan conversations as if people know or will discover my flaws. As I listen to them, I'm already on the defensive and tend to take whatever they say as though I am being personally attacked or criticized in some way.

When I'm defensive, it doesn't take much to hurt my feelings.

Sometimes, when I'm worried about my past failures, I may interrupt the speaker and say something like,

- "Those things always happen to me,"
- "I went through that same thing once."

When I take things personally, I may bring the conversation back to me and away from the speaker.

When I am overwhelmed by fear of failure, I automatically respond from a place of resignation. When I'm this afraid, you'll hear me say things like:

- "What's the use, we've tried it before and it didn't work."
- "We tried something similar and it didn't work so this won't work either."
- "There's no point, nothing ever changes around here."

When I scan conversations worried about my past failures and my flaws, I am defensive. People around me feel as if they are walking on egg shells and might even avoid me.

When I'm anxious about my time, I see you interrupting me as a threat.

When I'm protective of my time, I watch the clock as the other person speaks, willing them to get to the bottom line in four seconds or less.

When I feel pressed for time, I want the speaker to skip their story and get to the point.

When I'm threatened by you intruding on my time, I also tend to formulate my response, conclusion, decision, answer, or solution before the speaker has finished their first sentence.

There are many times I don't hear you. You may find yourself talking fast or stuttering over your words. You won't feel heard because you aren't.

Eventually, you'll stop talking to me, even if you have some information that could save my business, my marriage, or my relationship with my kids among other many other important things.

In each of the examples described above, notice fear's underlying motive. It seeks to dominate and control. Fear is power-hungry because it does not believe in its inherent value and worth.

Instead. The emotions stirred up enslave me in a consciousness of scarcity, lack, and limitation. I am no longer in the driver seat of my life when I am consumed by fear. Once it has taken over the wheel, I complain, rant and rave, or attempt to hide and disappear.

With this ugly emotion is at the helm, I feel a compulsion to control or dominate; in extreme cases, I may believe violence is the only solution to the problem. The good news is that with greater awareness of my fear triggers, I am better equipped to transcend the destructive impact fear has in my life.

The catch? When I don't like what I see on the outside, it's time to start examining what's happening with me on the inside.

What do *I* believe?

The Most Lethal Villains - Judgments & Beliefs

My judgments and beliefs have a significant impact on how much pain I am in and on how much I suffer. My judgments and beliefs affect how happy or unhappy I am.

What keeps me stuck in the soup bowl of life is that I am a judging and voting machine. In the blink of an eye, I have an opinion about everything. I agree with something, or I disagree with it. I automatically judge situations as either good or bad. I judge other people's opinions as right or wrong. I judge everything, and other people do this too.

The problem with this is that I inherited most of my judgments and beliefs. They came from:

- My family.
- My teachers, mentors and/or coaches.
- My close friends.
- My family's religious affiliation; or lack thereof.
- History.
- The news media.
- Societal and cultural customs and norms.
- Science.
- Doctors, experts, and other authorities.
- Political associations.
- The entertainment industry, and
- Other institutions.

Another problem with judgments is that we act as if our judgments are representative of the whole person. The reality is that they as a snapshot of that person in a single moment. Life is like a movie, and so are people.

Movies consist of many snapshots that form the whole story. If a person's life consists of 60 billion individual picture frames, and I judge that person based on three or four snapshots of who they are, I fail to appreciate the whole movie that person is.

Imagine what would happen if a parent judged a toddler's ability to walk after the first three or four steps. The toddler stands up and falls. The toddler takes one shaky step and falls again, and repeats this process.

If the parent judged the toddler's ability to walk based on those first few shaky steps, the parent would tell their toddler, "Hey kid, it doesn't look like you're getting the hang of this walking thing, so you might as well give up walking."

Most people can't fathom doing this to a toddler—yet we do it to ourselves and each other in the blink of an eye!

Over the years, I've discovered that my beliefs and judgments impact how much pain or happiness I experience in the following areas of my life:

- Self-image.
- Sense of well-being.
- Career.
- Finances.
- Health.
- Relationships.
- Peace of mind.
- Life purpose.
- Sense of satisfaction with life.

My Background Story

Beliefs and judgments are the ingredients that form the recipe of our personal life story. It's the story of who we are, how we came to be that way and why we are the way we are.

The problem is that most of us are living a story handed down to us rather than our own authentic story. To illustrate how powerful and sneaky the impact our inherited beliefs and judgments has on us, I'll share my personal life story:

To put things in a cultural context, I grew up in Georgia in the 1960s and 1970s, a time when most mothers stayed at home with the kids as most fathers went to work to support the family. Not so in my house. My mother was a pioneer. She worked full-time outside the home, as did my father.

I was also an only child. While my parents worked, I was placed in childcare. When I started first grade, the people I would come to consider my adopted grandparents kept me after school. Being in school was good for me. As an only child, I spent most of my time around adults, so school provided me with the opportunity for social interaction with kids my own age.

In my school and neighborhood, there was no diversity of ethnicities or cultures. As a Caucasian, I did not know a single person of African American, Native American, Hispanic, Asian, or any other ethnic background. Most adults around me did not trust anyone different than them. Most adults belittled anyone who appeared different (e.g., black people, hippies, The Beatles).

At a very young age, their belittling of anyone different than them did not make sense to me. In church, I was taught, and believed wholeheartedly, that God made us in God's own image. I asked, "Doesn't that mean in God's eyes we are equal?" Deep in my soul, despite the racism and bigotry in my family and around me, I believed that we are all created in the image of God. To me, that means we are equal in the eyes of God.

That belief allowed my heart to stay open to people from all walks of life, even when I didn't understand their traditions and customs. Unfortunately, I did not hold onto that belief when it came to me. When it came to me, I allowed my seeming differences to make me feel less than the beautiful likeness of God that I am.

I grew up in a home where my parents were not happy. The evidence I used to form this belief was based on how much they fought, and the way they would degrade each other when they fought. They called each other names, hurtful names. I knew the words they called each other hurt because they told me so, and it hurt me to hear it.

As I grew older, I heard a lot of, "Why is your mother that way, why can't she be more like <fill in the blank>" and, "Why is your father like that, why can't he be more <fill in the blank>." This message was delivered to me as well. I *often heard, "Why can't you be more like your cousin so and so?", "Why did you bring home a 98 on this test instead of a 100? If you hadn't missed that one question, you would have had a perfect score."*

Because I loved my parents so much, I mistakenly thought that it was my job to make them happy. Making them happy was a losing proposition, and my failure to do so left me feeling inadequate.

Fast forward several years.

For a long time, I knew I was different than most of the little girls my age. I didn't know how specifically. It was part that I was a tomboy, adventuresome, and an explorer in ways other little girls weren't, but there was something else, something that I could not explain that contributed to me feeling different.

In sixth grade, I figured it out. I discovered the word homo-sexual in the dictionary, and I knew what made me different. At first, I was elated because I'd figured it out! Immediately after feeling elated, I realized I was in a precarious situation. I knew that my parents and the church condemned homosexuality. I felt more alone than ever because I didn't know any other gay people. I couldn't talk to any grown-ups about it because they'd condemned me already.

More layers of not enough, not good enough, and never will be good enough got caked onto my psyche. It was apparent to me that no matter what, I was a failure. By the time I was 11 years old, I came to believe that the world would be a better place without me in it. I frequently contemplated suicide. I begged God to put an end to my life. I devised numerous ways to kill myself but failed to follow through on any of them. The fact of the matter is, as far as I've come, I have moments when I contemplate committing suicide.

By the Grace of God, I am still here.

The message from home to church to school and everywhere in between was clear.

I did not measure up.

I did not fit in.

I did not belong: it was more important to be liked and to fit in than it was to be true to who I am.

Like me, you are a product of the family and culture in which you were raised. In turn, you inherited certain judgments and beliefs about yourself, other people, and life.

You made up stories about yourself and the world, based on highly-charged emotional events. Some of that stuff serves you well, but other stuff keeps you from enjoying life.

Belief Formation

As I've worked to heal my pain and move beyond the stuff that prevents me from enjoying the best life possible. I discovered some beliefs that drain me of any chance of happiness and perpetuate my pain. I also discovered some beliefs that enhance my well-being, optimizing my sense of happiness and fulfillment in life.

While it's true that I inherited most of my judgments and beliefs, *I also discovered that there is no power in blaming my past or anyone else for my current situation.*

I've discovered the true power is using these negative experiences and people to point me in a better direction. This amazing power to heal my pain and be happy lies in my ability to use the stuff that does not work as a guide for which beliefs I need to change.

I use what doesn't work to clarify what does so that I will develop beliefs that serve me better. The more proficient I get at this, the better I feel, and the better my results.

On the path toward healing my pain, I learned that beliefs are formed by:

- What we were repeatedly told as children.
- An opinion we form, or a judgment we make during a highly-charged emotional event.
- What we tell ourselves time and time again.
- What we agree with that other people talk about continually.
- What we agree with that people in authority tell us.
- What we unconsciously absorb from the news, television, radio, movies, the internet, social media, and other avenues of information every day.

The four key elements to forming beliefs are:

- Repetition.
- Emotionallycharged events.
- Giving authority to others.
- Unconscious absorption.

Belief Analysis

Once I learned how beliefs are formed, I discovered the importance of examining what I believe now against what has been handed down to me.

To conduct a thorough analysis of what I believe, I asked myself what I truly believe about forty-two things. A short list of the areas I examined includes: what I believe about: myself, family, work, money, happiness, peace, fun, religion, violence, power, beauty, health, weight, success, and failure. (For the full Belief Inventory refer to the appendix.)

This Belief Inventory helped me uncover which beliefs contribute to my pain, and those which empower me to feel better.

As I conducted my Belief Inventory, I asked myself what I had been taught about each area. It didn't matter so much *who* taught me to believe a certain way as much as *what* I had been taught.

I asked a simple question: does this support me in being as happy as I can be?

For instance, my parents had a great work ethic: show up early, give every job your best effort, and pay attention to details. Those behaviors stemmed from their belief about what it meant to be a good employee, and what it meant to succeed in the workforce. Those beliefs have served me very well.

They also had the belief that the best way to make it in the world was to go to work for a good company and retire with a gold watch. That model worked well for the two of them in the cultural climate they lived in.

For me, not so much. The workforce climate I live in had changed. The loyalty that companies once had toward their employees had evaporated. Layoffs and downsizing were the descriptors of the workforce I experienced. To hinge my career happiness on the same formula my parents did might have led to disaster. Entrepreneurialism has been a far better formula for my happiness.

I also looked at how things were going in each area. If things were going well and adding to my happiness, I observed the beliefs that contributed to the positive outcomes I achieved.

If I was in pain over how things were going for me in any area, I knew there were some beliefs I needed to change. For example, I discovered that if I wanted to make the contribution I hoped to, I needed to heal the belief that I'm worthless. If I wanted to be more prosperous, I needed to heal my beliefs about scarcity, lack, and not enough to go around.

With each belief, I also asked myself, "Is this true?"

If there were people in the world doing well in an area I wasn't doing well in, I knew I was missing something. I knew that it was likely that one of the unconscious beliefs I'd absorbed was having a negative impact on my happiness and my potential.

I found it invaluable to decipher which beliefs cause me pain and which ones make me feel more hopeful and optimistic. I am happier than I've ever been and notice that deep down, on a day-to-day basis, I remain happy.

When I notice that I'm not as happy as I want to be, I work to uncover the judgment or belief that is contributing to my pain and unhappiness. Once I know this, I can shift myself in a more positive and happier direction.

As you conduct your own Belief Inventory, you'll find some beliefs that serve you well, and add to your enjoyment of life.

You'll also find some beliefs that cause you pain.

The good news is that the more you are aware of what **you** believe, the wider the doors open for you to experience feeling better than ever and to achieving better results in your life.

The Number One Killer of Happiness

Along the way, I also discovered the number one killer of my happiness. This one is a deadly toxic belief, hopped up on steroids. I referred to it earlier in the Introduction: It's called *being right*.

What makes being right so lethal?

Next time you speak to someone, notice what happens when they insist that they are right about something, particularly when you don't agree with them. How do you feel? Where do you go? What do you do?

When someone insists that they are right, there's no room for anyone else or anything else to show up. Something detrimental happens to me too when I insist that I'm right.

When I'm right, I make other people wrong. Making other people wrong creates a win-lose situation which ultimately causes everyone to lose. When you think about it, do you like it when somebody makes you feel bad and wrong?

Me neither!

Other than feeling the yucky pain associated feeling bad and wrong, there is another huge negative result to being right. Being right fails to account for the Big Picture.

My point of view is only one, based on my limited personal experience. While my experience is valuable, it does not include every experience available in the universe.

It serves me better to remember the story of the Blind Men and the Elephant adapted from a poem by John Godfrey Saxe:

The Blind Men and the Elephant

Six blind men reached out to define what being an elephant means.

The first blind man placed his hands on the elephant's broad and sturdy side, and decided that elephants were very much like walls.

As the second blind man felt the sharp tip and roundness of elephant's tusk, he was convinced that elephants were like spears.

The third blind man grasped the elephant's squirming trunk. To him, an elephant was akin to a snake.

The fourth blind man's hands fell at the elephant's knee, and he boldly declared that elephants resembled a mighty tree.

With his hands landing on the elephant's ear, the fifth blind man decided that elephants were like fluttering fans.

The sixth blind man seized the elephant's tail and made the leap that elephants were like a rope.

The blind men argued loud and long. Each convinced his opinion was the right one, though in truth each man was partly right and partly wrong.

Moral: Often in theological wars, we argue that we are right in complete ignorance of what others see and mean. We argue about elephants not one of us has seen.

The story of the blind men and the elephant reminds me that I only see one small portion of the Big Picture. When I insist that my judgments and beliefs are right, I become blind.

When I insist that I'm right about something, my righteousness acts as a blindfold, preventing me from seeing the Big Picture. Getting sucked into such a small world view intensifies the amount of pain I'm in, interfering with my ability to enjoy life.

What would make you feel better?

- What needs do you have that are not adequately met (e.g., basic survival, safety and security, love and belonging, esteem, self-actualization)?
- How is sneaky fear affecting you? Your relationships? Your work? Your dreams?
- Are you suffering from any of the symptoms of sneaky fear?
- Are you on any positions?
- What are you scanning for in conversations (e.g., looking good, failure, time)? In life?
- What are you scanning for when life throws you a curve ball?
- What are you afraid to say because of your concerns about looking good?
- What and/or who do you complain about most?
- Are you willing to pay attention to your judgments and get off them in favor of a greater possibility/reward (e.g., the toddler learning to walk)?

- Assess your pain-happiness level in each of the following areas (with zero meaning extremely painful and seven meaning extremely happy):
  - Self-image.
  - Sense of well-being.
  - Career.
  - Finances.
  - Health.
  - Relationships.
  - Peace of mind.
  - Life purpose.
  - Sense of satisfaction with life.
- Are you measuring your level of pain and happiness based on judgments and a belief handed down to you by others, or is your assessment based on your own firsthand experience?
- Is it possible that beliefs handed down to you contribute to the way you experience life?
- What's your personal life story (e.g., the story of who you are, how you came to be that way and why you are the way you are)?
- Is your personal life story full of drama and upsets?
- Have you completed a thorough Belief Inventory?
- Have you identified which beliefs cause you pain, and which beliefs empower you to feel better? Remember, it *doesn't* matter who taught you to believe what you believe. What matters most is whether your beliefs support you in feeling as good as you can feel.
- How are things going for you in each area of your life (e.g., family, relationships, health, career/business, finances)?
- What beliefs serve you well?
- Which beliefs would you benefit from changing?
- Are there people in the world doing well in an area you aren't doing well in?

- What are you being right about (e.g., your boss, your employees, your spouse, your ex, your brother/sister, your aunt/uncle, your children, your coworkers, people, the President)?
- Which part of the elephant do you see?

Chapter 2

The Second Courageous Practice –
Ramping Up Your Power

Becoming Superman - Moving Beyond Fear and Limiting Beliefs

Armed with the knowledge that we inherited most of our judgments and beliefs and recognizing how being right keeps us stuck in our pain, we now have an appreciation of where we are.

The Belief Inventory enables us to take a balcony view of our lives. Standing on the balcony allows us to gaze out at the soup we're in and glean vital information about how to turn things around in our favor.

Most of us have experienced sadness, remorse, and disappointment over a choice we made. We've made choices we regret. We've made mistakes. At one time or another, most of us have done something that resulted in undesirable consequences.

When this happens, it erodes our trust, our trust in ourselves, and our trust in each other. Lack of trust breeds fear and doubt which fuels our upsets, thereby intensifying our pain. We feel disempowered.

When we feel disconnected from our power in life, we die a slow painful death. Bit-by-bit, breath-by-breath, we lose sight of the power housed inside our authentic self. We allow our fear-based beliefs to keep us running nowhere on the treadmill of life as our hearts ache for relief from our pain.

Some people are in so much pain that they overcompensate for their fear acting overly confident and aggressive. They do their best to intimidate others because they are afraid that this is the only way to get what they want. However, this is not real power.

This is fear power.

Fear at its worst brings out bullying behavior, causing people to build fences designed to keep others out or weapons designed to destroy one's perceived enemies.

When we are this afraid, we have no power to solve the challenge we face, because we cannot see possibilities that work for all parties involved.

When we are this scared, we forget that win-lose situations result in *everyone* losing.

When we are this fearful, we think: "If I kill my enemy, I win," instead of realizing that killing leads to more killing.

It takes *more* courage to choose not to lash out in fear, and instead to purposefully attempt to gain a better appreciation for what it's like in the other person or group's world.

It takes *more* courage to reach out in compassion than it does to build walls and kill people.

Some people are in so much pain that they overcompensate for their fear by hiding. Rather than participate fully in life and risk looking foolish, they hang out on the sidelines watching the game of life.

People overwhelmed by fear in this way are the ones who constantly focus on the risks and dangers associated with doing things. These are the folks who use their imagination to create the worst possible scenario. They use their worries to excuse themselves from taking the risks associated with dancing with the unknown.

Some people are convinced the unknown is dangerous. The unknown is neither good nor bad; it's simply the unknown. People whose fear has them hiding want you to come and hide too.

If you pursue your dreams while they sit on the sidelines, what does that say about them? You might make them feel wrong about the dangers they feared, and they might feel foolish for not taking risks.

The second courageous practice moves us beyond our fear and our limiting beliefs by transforming us into our own superhero.

It requires us to ask one new question, make one essential choice and take one consistent action.

One New Question

Many people stay stuck in their pain because they focus on this question: "Why me?" Why me is a *victim* question. The terrible things that happened to you and to me are not personal. There are billions of valid reasons why something happened. Here are a few:

- When my dad's mom abandoned him, his father beat him so that's why my dad abused me.
- My family has always been poor.
- Being obese is genetic, it runs in my family.
- People leave me because I think I am unlovable..
- I did not get the promotion because they don't like me.

Our reasons do not alleviate our pain. Asking "why?" keeps us stuck in our pain because what we agree and disagree with owns us. With this mentality, the reason why becomes the driving force for our actions and for our excuses. Asking why perpetuates the victim mentality, keeping us stuck in the pain cycle.

Consider this: If I were to give you an airplane model kit and ask you to assemble it, you would expect to create a replica of an airplane, not an orangutan.

You don't question this.

When you assemble the kit, you expect it to result in an airplane because you know what the model was designed to produce. Models only allow us to create what the model was intended to create or replicate.

Role models are people you admire, people who have something you want to have, people you want to emulate. Sometimes, we jump to this conclusion without understanding the model our role models are following.

For example, what is your model for being successful?

What is your model for being healthy?

What is your model for healing your pain and overcoming the challenges in your life?

How well are those models working for you?

Are they producing the results you want, or are you still hurting?

If you are still in pain, your model is not working for you. Fear is getting the best of you because you are too afraid to seek out a new model. Our fear-based beliefs keep our hearts bloodied and battered. Our anxiety causes us to contract and close our hearts and minds in a feeble attempt to stay safe or avoid more pain.

The good news is there is a way out of the pain cycle. Next, I'll discuss two practices that will help you feel better and ramp up your personal power so that you achieve better results.

Shifting from Pain to Power

The first practice involves shifting from your pain toward your power. To reclaim your power, stop asking "Why?" Instead, ask *what would I rather see?*

When I ask myself: "What would I rather see?" I shift my focus away from the pain and toward something better.

Where my attention and focus goes, my energy flows.

Even if I don't know how to achieve the better thing I imagine, keeping this question in mind serves as a lighthouse, beckoning me to new shores and experiences.

Once you are clear about what you would rather see, ask yourself: What does one have to believe to experience this thing that I want to experience? For example, several years ago, I got caught up in the budget cuts and downsizing trend that many people experienced in the workplace. It was not easy going to work each day and wondering if my position would be eliminated.

My financial health and well-being was at risk. However, with the encouragement and prayers of some good friends, I did not allow myself to get caught up in the fear that seemed to run rampant around me.

Instead, I started affirming what I wanted.

Internally, I claimed my ideal job repeatedly. I wrote a simple description of it on an index card that I carried with me at all times. When I felt afraid, I pulled out the index card with the affirmative prayer for my ideal job and gave thanks for it as if it were already my job.

What took place was a series of divine incidents in which God propelled me closer and closer to my ideal job. I went from one great job to a better one over the span of about eight years. Throughout the entire eight-year time span, I did not get laid off or downsized. It was a matter of one great door opening for me after another.

That's the power of focusing on what I'd rather see and experience.

I still write my ideal situation on index cards and read them frequently, especially when I'm afraid or have been in a group of negative people. I do this because I recognize how important it is to repeat the new empowering belief throughout the day.

I encourage you to develop a similar practice. Imagine how you will feel when you accomplish the thing you want to accomplish: visualize it now. Find photos and/or words that represent the images of how you want to be seen, and how you want your life to unfold.

Put those words and photos in places you will see them throughout the day (i.e., put images or words in your daily calendar, make a vision board or PowerPoint presentation out of them and view them at least 3-4 times each day, and set phone alarms throughout the day with keywords that trigger your vision).

As you tend to the garden of your new beliefs, you'll find that you feel better and get more of what you want out of life. Better beliefs equal better, freer living.

One Essential Choice

The next shifting from pain to power practice involves an essential choice. This is a choice you must make, moment-by-moment, if you want to break free from the pain cycle and live an empowered life.

To move beyond your pain and toward the life you aspire to enjoy, it's imperative that you *decide to trust yourself and tell the truth about your experience.*

Too often, we allow our pain to interfere with our ability to trust. Lack of trust escalates our pain. We think that because something bad happened, we can't be trusted, or other people can't be trusted. We forget that we are here to learn and grow.

Deciding to trust yourself does not mean you will not make another mistake again or that everything automatically goes in your favor. Trusting yourself does not mean you won't feel bad again. Deciding to trust yourself means that you are confident that you will learn what you need to learn from your current situation to improve your future.

When you decide to trust yourself, you reclaim your personal power. Instead of giving your power away to the events that happen, you will trust yourself to take positive action on your behalf or on behalf of another. When you trust yourself, you'll notice that you have less drama in your life.

Drama may visit you, but often it won't be your drama. That's because when you decide to trust yourself, you stop blaming other people for your circumstances.

When you trust yourself, you know that you will take positive steps to get yourself out of the situations that do not work for you and into what does work for you. The more you practice taking positive steps to improve your lot in life, the better you feel.

Honesty

Shifting toward what works better requires you to be honest with yourself. What underlying belief contributed to the situation you are in now?

Are you willing to take responsibility for making the changes you need to make?

Are you willing to take responsibility for asking for what you want and need, and to keep asking for it until you get it?

Are you willing to let go of toxic people and places to have your life work?

I've known couples who stay together because their relationship is familiar to them even though they are miserable. It's too scary to step out into the unknown singles world. I've also known people who prefer the comfort of their misery rather than having their life work.

These are the folks that love our sympathy and receive a huge payoff whenever we feel sorry for them and give them our attention. The miserable person doesn't care if the attention we pour out to them is positive (i.e., you poor dear), or negative (i.e., knock it off, you life-sucking vampire). The miserable person is too busy being right about being a victim to do what they need to do to make their life work.

The choice is ours to make.

Play for what we want and trust that we will get there so long as we keep learning, or stay stuck in the familiar pain, agony, and despair of drama. People who choose the latter have decided they can't be trusted, and they will not trust you either no matter how hard you try to earn their trust. That's why the drama story has survived for so many centuries.

The Marathon Perspective

Deciding to trust myself means I trust myself to work toward creating what I want to see and experience. As I work toward this, I am better served by looking at life as a marathon instead of a sprint race.

A woman I know shared her secret for completing three marathons. She said, "The marathon is one idea that takes approximately 10,000 steps to successfully complete." That's 10,000 or more actions that need to be executed successfully to realize the one idea called a marathon.

From the marathon perspective, I'm in it for the long haul. I might strike out today, but my commitment helps me learn from what did not work today. I also learn from what did work. Each day I stay in the marathon race I come closer to victory even though the finish line may not be in sight.

From a marathon viewpoint, I begin to understand that things are not what they seem. Things are not forever fixed as they might appear to be. Taking a marathon outlook, I see movement and fluidity. I see beyond the upper edge of the soup bowl. From this place, I step into what I call my highest and best self. When I'm at my highest and best, I trust myself and I am empowered.

You and I are best served by deciding to trust ourselves and by telling the truth about our experience. I feel better and get better results when I trust myself and take personal responsibility for the part I played in how events unfold, and you will too.

Sometimes I blow it, and there's something I need to clean up to achieve the results I want.

At other times, I let my stuff get the best of me and I create damage in a relationship. When this occurs, I do my best to clean up the damage I created.

The more you practice taking responsibility for yourself and the results you achieve, the better you'll feel and the better results you'll get. You and I are fully capable of trusting ourselves to succeed at creating a life that works.

Make and Keep Agreements

Developing trust requires courage. The decision itself is brave, as telling the truth about our experience requires fearlessness. The very act of lifting the veil to uncover the underlying beliefs that limit us requires some guts.

Once we've discovered our limiting beliefs, it takes fortitude to make new agreements that empower us, and it takes determination to keep those agreements as we go about our lives each day.

For example, I discovered that my underlying belief about not being good enough was wreaking havoc in my romantic relationships. Acting out of this belief caused me to engage in behaviors that were destructive to my relationships.

Equipped with this new awareness, I made an agreement with myself to work diligently at changing this belief. Whenever ideas that I'm not good enough or worthless float through my brain, I consciously affirm my worth and my value. I consciously elect to let go of the self-doubt.

I choose to trust that if the person I'm with has not told me I'm not enough for them, then our relationship is okay. By making and keeping this agreement with myself, I feel better about me and I've got far better results.

Opposition to Results

It takes courage to recognize our opposition to results. Sometimes that opposition is ourselves and the limiting beliefs we've inherited. Sometimes, the opposition we face is from other people.

In either case, it takes courage to stop playing the blame game, to stop making other people bad and wrong, and to take ownership of our life.

The more we choose to trust ourselves to keep playing for what works, the better we feel and the more authentically powerful we become.

Positions and Their Payoffs

From a learning orientation, I am well equipped to discover my positions and their payoffs. I recognize I'm in a position, or being right, when I:

- Make someone else wrong.
- Make myself wrong.
- Am being right about anything.
- Do not feel powerful in that area of my life.

I also detect that I'm in a position when I'm inauthentic or hiding something, and when I attempt to dominate or control someone. Some of the most common payoffs for being right are:

- People let me off the hook, they don't expect me to change so I get to stay small.
- The illusion of safety that playing small brings me.
- Attention.
- Validation even if it's toxic for me.
- I get to dominate and feel in control.
- I think I look good to others.
- I think it relieves my fear.
- I think it gives me power over another person.

The problem is being stuck in a position causes me to lose in the game of life. My perceptions cost me by killing my aliveness and my connection with others. My outlook costs me happiness, satisfaction, and peace of mind. When I'm on a position, I lose my power.

My attitude acts like a cage that enslaves me, eroding the fabric of my freedom. This view keeps me stuck in feeling bad, self-righteous, regretful, angry, disappointed, shameful and guilty because deep inside I know I am capable of far greater things than the silly coffin my stance puts me in.

It takes tremendous courage for me to adjust my outlook. Changing my position requires me to acknowledge that my perceptions and beliefs about what happened may be incorrect.

It takes courage to stop portraying others as bad and wrong and to acknowledge that they are doing what makes sense to them given their experience, vantage point, and present awareness.

It takes tremendous courage to take the needle out of our arm and give up being right in favor of what works.

It takes remarkable courage to make the overarching goal and mission of our lives to be choosing what works.

Choosing What Works

Choosing what works requires me to:

- Communicate what I need to say (e.g., stop withholding communication and/or hiding out).
- Communicate my role in the situation and take responsibility for what I did and for what does not work.
- Communicate what I've learned and any promises and commitments I'm willing to make based on what I learned.

Creating a life that works means I look out for me and I also daringly explore how I can support others in having their lives work too. As I bravely communicate my goal of support to others, I find out what's needed or wanted and to the best of my ability I start doing it.

This often requires me to pay attention to any detrimental elements that pop up around my goal of support and to handle them. For example, when a disagreement occurs, I ask the other party what would work better for them, share what would work for me better, and do my best to keep choice in for the people involved.

Creating a trust-based life that works also means that I am willing to be supported, not rescued, by others. Sometimes I can't tell when I'm in the soup bowl of life being bashed around by subconscious limiting beliefs. Sometimes other people support me by sharing their observations or by offering me support in some other tangible way (e.g., design my website for me, connect me with a mentor or other expert).

Accepting support gets me back up on the balcony. Being supported also shows people that they mean something to me and I value them.

The more I pay attention, strengthen positive results, and adjust for diminished results, the better I feel and the more life works. I realize what some essential part of me knew: I can trust myself. Yet, I will not trust myself if I don't demand of myself that I persevere.

One Consistent Action: Persevere

I've learned it's about perseverance when it comes to gaining mastery at anything in life. Firefighters persist until the fire is put out. They don't stop fighting the fire because there are obstacles in their way. They may back off momentarily to regroup and re-strategize, but they persist in their efforts until the fire is out.

It's easy to quit when things get hard and when we face seemingly insurmountable opposition. We allow our discomfort and fear to talk us out of pursuing our dreams. To feel better and get better results, we must persevere in the direction our hearts call us to pursue until we reach the destination that fulfills our soul.

As much as I wanted to be a firefighter, I would have flunked out of rookie school if I hadn't persevered. At the Fire Academy, recruits participate in drills designed to prepare us to be successful firefighters.

The Fire Academy is a safe place to learn because conditions are carefully controlled, but that doesn't mean I did not get scared. What follows are two simple stories of perseverance that led to me making my dream to be a firefighter come true.

I know that if I persevere, you can too!

Using Breath to Overcome Fear and Perseverance

Firefighting taught me a lot about dealing with physical danger and keeping my fear in check. One of my greatest lessons on this subject occurred during rookie school.

When I was a rookie in the Fire Academy, we were required to participate in a training drill. The drill required us to climb up the inside stairwell of our training tower while carrying a fifty-pound section of fire hose in full turnout gear with an estimated weight of forty pounds.

No biggie.

The thing that upped the ante in this drill was that our face mask was blacked out. We were expected to perform various firefighting maneuvers in complete darkness. For the duration of the drill, we were blind.

This drill was timed, and we used our air tanks. Failure to complete the drill in the allotted amount of time, or running out of air meant failing the drill and risking getting kicked out of the Fire Academy. Does this sound scary? The actual drills themselves did not frighten me. We completed similar drills, and I felt confident I could handle this one.

That day, my training instructor marched my blinded self into the bottom stairwell of the training tower. I was fine until I heard the heavy metal clank of the door shutting behind me. I found myself in complete darkness. I could not see so much as a shadow.

Hearing the loud clank of the heavy metal door shut, engulfed in complete darkness, my so-called confidence evaporated into thin air. I couldn't see anything. How was I supposed to carry the hose up four flights of stairs when I couldn't see a thing?

At that precise moment, I remember feeling utterly alone. I had no idea how I was going to carry the hose up those stairs in complete darkness. As my heart pounded and my breath rate increased, I sounded like Darth Vader running for Olympic gold.

The sound of my rapid breathing set alarm bells off in my head. I needed to gain immediate control of my fear if I stood a chance of completing this drill.

In that moment, in the pitch-black darkness of the stairwell, completely alone, I came face to face with the fear of not knowing if I could do something, also known as the fear of failure.

Thankfully, some of our earlier training kicked in. I begin to focus on slowing my breath rate.

Breathe s-l-o-w-l-y.

Slowing my breathing led me to a place of internal calmness. From this calmer state, I heard the answer to my question about how to complete this drill in complete darkness.

The answer was simple: one step at a time.

A simple story, yet a powerful lesson that served me well in my firefighting career, especially when I faced situations far more dangerous than an empty stairwell under zero fire conditions.

It was a powerful lesson that served me well in life. When I get scared, it's time for me to slow down, breathe, and take things one step at a time.

Focusing on my breath calms me. It also connects to me to that still, small voice within so I hear the wisdom it offers me. I also believe conscious breathing connects me to my Source, or what I call God. This connection to Source helps me tap into the wisdom of the universe.

K-12 Rescue Saw

An important part of firefighting is timeliness and mechanical ability. We are timed as we practice using tools and equipment under controlled conditions, so that under fire conditions, we aren't bumbling around.

As a part of my training, I had to crank a saw. Not just any saw, but a K-12 fire rescue saw. I had already mastered the chainsaw, but the K-12 fire rescue saw was kicking my butt. I couldn't get the darn thing started to save my life.

I'd come so far—farther than any other woman in the process, but was this saw going to send my firefighting career up in smoke?

I was under a lot of pressure at the time, as were my peers. Many otherswere curious to see if a woman could make it. I was scrutinized by my instructors and classmates, the medics, the county commissioners, the reporters, and the citizens.

With safe operating procedures in mind, my instructor and the guys cranked the saw using a specific technique. Since it worked for them, it should have worked for me, but it didn't.

No matter how hard I tried or how many times I tried, the darn saw wouldn't start. I tried so hard that I pulled a muscle and severely bruised my entire forearm. Even injured, I tried, and tried, and tried, and couldn't get the K-12 saw to start.

Fortunately, I had an instructor who was more interested in my success than my failure. This instructor gave me multiple opportunities to practice. Monday through Friday during each break I'd practice. He stayed with me each day after class for about 30 minutes allowing me to practice cranking the K-12 fire rescue saw.

I don't remember how long this went on, most likely a couple of weeks, though at the time my injured forearm made it seem like each day's practice session took a year. My instructor coached me and together we explored new ways for me to crank the K-12 saw safely until I did it!

While I was learning to crank the K-12 fire rescue saw, some of my male counterparts ribbed me good-naturedly. I heard a few others talking about me behind my back; these were the few that did not think a woman belonged in the Fire Department. These few wanted me to fail.

Despite the difficulty I faced cranking that damn saw, I persevered. I learned to crank the K-12 fire rescue saw safely, successfully, consistently, and quickly. I completed my training, graduated, and achieved my dream of being a firefighter.

Persistence pays.

You already have what it takes to persist. Perseverance yields tremendous payoffs. It makes dreams come true, even dreams that seem far-fetched and outlandishly out there.

What Would Make You Feel Better?

- Where have you let yourself down in life?
- Is fear power getting the best of you in any area of your life? If so, what are you willing to do to gain the upper hand over fear power so you can step into your authentic power?
- Are you willing to feel powerful in life?
- When you experience drama and/or get upset, are you willing to pause and attempt to gain an appreciation for what it's like in the other person's world?
- What walls have you erected that reaching out courageously with compassion might tear down?

- Who have you killed off (i.e., what relationships have you severed), and how might you reach out courageously with compassion to mend the divisiveness between you and the other party?

- In what areas of your life are you sitting on the sidelines?

- Are you willing to risk looking foolish and/or failing to gain the additional information you need to succeed?

- Are you willing to step courageously into the unknown?

- Are you willing to stop asking: "Why me?" and ask: "What would I rather see?"

- If life isn't working for you in an area, what would you rather see? What do people who are successful in that area believe?

- Are you willing to trust yourself moment-by-moment?

- How honest are you with yourself and others? Hint: The key to assessing how well you are doing here is by how well your life is working in each area.

- What new agreements do you need to make with yourself and/or the significant people in your life? How will you ensure you keep your agreements?

- Do you recognize your opposition to getting the results you want? How will you manage your opposition to getting the results you want?

- What are your positions and what are their payoffs? What has this cost you?

- How will you strengthen what works?

- Are you willing to persevere until you see that which you want to see and experience?

Chapter 3

The Third Courageous Practice – Playing to Strengths

The third courageous practice involves playing to your strengths and to the strengths of the people around you. I was indoctrinated into this practice when I became a member of the Fire Service. Firefighter units are some of the most effective teams I have ever encountered.

One of the things that make them so effective is the way firefighters play off each individual member of the team's strengths. Playing to one's strengths means taking an honest inventory of what a specific individual does well, even excels at. It also means taking an honest look at that specific individual's weaknesses—but not in a judgmental way.

Putting together a team this way strengthens the team and promotes success.

Identifying Strengths

As my county's first female firefighter, one thing was clear. I did *not* have the brute strength that my male counterparts had. I was strong and capable of doing what the job required, but I did not have the superior upper body strength that my fellow firefighters had.

However, I *did* have something the guys didn't.

I fitted into confined spaces better than they did because I was smaller. I tested the strength of floors compromised from the fire because I did not weigh as much. I also came in handy whenever we were called out to render medical assistance to females who had been raped. I did well comforting children traumatized from an emergency.

On the other hand, many of my male counterparts were better equipped at handling tasks that required superior upper body strength (e.g., busting through heavy metal doors, lifting extremely obese people entrapped in vehicles involved in car crashes, and lifting heavy loads of debris off people trapped underneath).

One guy was a genius at teaching fire behavior, an essential concept to succeed at fighting fires, but he did not have the common sense required to maneuver through a burning building safely. By placing him at the Fire Academy, we benefited from his brilliance and we were safer. Another guy had superior strength and acted as a one-man demolition team, but he did not handle the sight of blood very well.

The point is that each member of the team had things they excelled at, and things that weren't so easy for them to do. By playing to each other's strengths, we were much more effective than we would have been otherwise.

Address Weaknesses

To optimize our performance, it is equally important to address our weaknesses. No one is great at everything. We excel at some things and we are challenged by others. If the sight of blood makes you squeamish and causes you to faint, you would not make the best paramedic, nurse, or doctor. If sitting behind a desk drives you crazy, you would not make the best administrative assistant or computer programmer. If dealing with children makes you want to pull your hair out, you would not do well as a teacher or a stay-at-home parent.

What makes it difficult for us to acknowledge our weaknesses is that we think that doing so makes us look bad, inferior, stupid, or incompetent. We think being weak robs us of our power. Acknowledging my weaknesses does not make me less powerful; rather it empowers me to figure out how to get those needs addressed more effectively.

For instance, when you have a plumbing issue, you don't call an electrician to fix it. This also applies to hiring someone with the gift of gab to do your marketing instead of hiring a shy, introverted more technologically talented individual. One will bring business to your door while the other will make sure your computers and equipment allow you to provide your services effectively—but you would not want to reverse their roles.

Notice how we have certain adjectives to describe someone who is strong and different ones to describe someone who is weak. Our language is ripe with judgment, and we tend to place ourselves in the category we think will make us successful so that we look good—and so other people will like us.

We have a double standard.

When someone appears to have all their stuff together, we find it difficult to relate and connect with them. This is because perfection is inauthentic. The best way to receive the love and acceptance we thirst for is by being authentic. As we show others our true selves, perceived flaws and all, we also come closer to reaching our full potential.

When I acknowledge my strengths and weaknesses, I get to choose what activities I invest my energy and time doing, which skills and gifts I want to develop, and which tasks I am better served by finding someone else to do them for me. This empowers me to make a better use of my time, talents, attention, money, and resources.

Putting It into Practice

When I first joined the Fire Department, we had more fire units and firefighters than ambulances and medics. We also responded to more medical emergencies than we did fire emergencies. As a rookie firefighter, I found myself on medical calls administering the high-level first aid training I was taught at the Fire Academy.

As we waited for an ambulance to arrive on the scene, I hated not being able to do more for the patient. Recognizing that I lacked certain skills, I decided to go to school to become a Basic Emergency Medical Technician.

There are times in life when going back to school or taking classes to address a weakness is well-advised. However, I am terrible at fixing my computers and other electronic devices when they break. Whenever I talk to people who are experts in that area, my eyes glaze over and my ears shut down. I don't speak geek, I'm not a techie, and I have no desire to become an expert in this area.

I know that when my computer goes on the blink, I need to find someone more knowledgeable about computers to help me. This saves me tons of frustration, time, and aggravation. It allows me to leverage the skills of an expert in that area and their strengths. This approach gets me *out* of the pain cycle and enhances my sense of personal power.

Bearing this in mind, ask yourself the following questions:

- What are my strengths?
- What am I naturally good at?
- What do people tell me I'm good at?
- What do people ask me to do for them?
- What jobs have I excelled in?
- What am I doing when I lose track of time?
- What activities engage me the most?

Once you've assessed your strengths, ask yourself these questions:

- In a non-judgmental way, what are my weaknesses?
- What areas do I want and/or need to improve?
- What am I currently responsible for doing that I'd rather hire someone else to do for me?
- What responsibilities do I hate when it comes to making sure that it gets done—things that I find myself dragging my feet and dreading the thought ofdoing?

- What have people told me I'm no good at?
- What do I ask people to help me with most often?

After you've finished answering these questions for yourself, you may want to see if other people in your life are willing to engage in this strength and weakness assessment.

The key here is to collaborate in an honest, non-judgmental way.

Of course, there is nothing to stop you from identifying their strengths on your own and playing to their strengths, with or without their participation in this activity. Whether you gain people's cooperation or not, ask yourself how will you play to the strengths of:

- Your family members.
- Your friends.
- Your coworkers.
- Your boss.
- Your children.
- Your employees.

What kind of support might you offer to address their areas of perceived weakness?

Example of Informally Playing to Strengths

We wanted to install new flooring in our home. To save money, we opted to install the flooring ourselves with the help of a friend. Each member of the three-person team had their own strengths. While we did not formally identify each other's strengths, we naturally gravitated toward the tasks we excelled at.

One member was adept at measuring and cutting the flooring boards. Another person's strength was installing the boards over large areas. The third was good at the detailed work required in tight spaces. As each member performed the tasks they excelled in, the project was completed quickly, efficiently, and with excellent results.

Example of Formally Playing to Strengths and Addressing Weaknesses

Sometimes good people and good teams get stuck. When this happens, performance decreases and the amount of internal bickering and disagreements increase. Case in point:

> *I once worked on a consulting project where two key groups of people needed to combine their efforts to achieve optimal results. Neither group felt like they could trust the other group.*
>
> *Their distrust of one another lead to a lot of anger, political positioning, and backbiting which created even more suspicion. This resulted in them not sharing the critical information needed to produce the results both parties wanted.*
>
> *As consultants, our team listened to both party's objections. We teased out their concerns about sharing information we knew was vital to the project's success, andwe assessed each group's strengths and weaknesses.*
>
> *We recognized that trust between the two groups needed to be nurtured for the project to succeed. We brought both parties together. We began by focusing on the common goal both parties shared, which was to save lives. We acknowledged what each group did well, and how each group's contribution was necessary to save lives.*
>
> *We showcased the role each party needed to play for a positive result to occur. We then asked each individually why they needed the information they had requested and asked them to share how that related to saving lives.*
>
> *The clarity this process provided enabled each group to begin trusting the other, overcoming the weakness of distrust. They gained an appreciation of each other's strengths and finally shared the information needed to realize their*

collective goal, which significantly improved their ability to save lives.

In the above example, our team reminded both parties of their common goal. We highlighted each group's strengths.

Our team also addressed their weaknesses, or the upsets, that prevented them from achieving their shared goal.

Upsets wreak havoc in our relationships, create stress in our lives, and interfere with our progress as we strive to achieve our goals. To get the best results in life, we need to address our upsets.

Upsets

We get upset when we fear that what we want to happen won't happen. Fear creates stress and tension in our bodies and pain in our psyches. Pain over our upsets pollutes the environment around us (e.g., think of organizations or people that feel stifling to you). Upsets lead to most of the relationship failures we experience.

Upsets consist of the following elements: a thwarted intention, an unfulfilled expectation, and a withheld or undelivered communication.

Thwarted Intention

"The road to hell is paved with good intentions."

There are two popular interpretations of this age-old quote. The first is that a good intention may have unintended and negative consequences. The second is that a person may have the intention of engaging in a good action but fails to follow through with that action.

Examples of thwarted intentions include:

- Intending to lose weight by the wedding, but not losing it.
- Intending to quit smoking, but not getting around to it yet.

- Intending to call Aunt Martha, but putting it off and not getting to speak with her before she died.
- Wanting something to go a certain way and it not going that way.
- Planning a big surprise party for one's sweetheart, only to discover the sweetheart did not like being surprised.
- Intending to help your child tie her shoe, but she got angry and shouted, "No! I can do this all by myself."
- Intending for a new business venture to succeed, but going bankrupt.

Once I figure out that a thwarted intention is the root cause of an upset, I am in a better position to resolve that upset. When my good intentions have unintended negative consequences, I find it best to view the situation as a learning opportunity.

I get curious and ask the affected party what specifically didn't work for them and what would work better. I then do my best to do what they told me would work better.

When I am at the brunt of someone else's good intentions, I do my best to forgive. I'm honest. I've learned that we teach people how to treat us. I tell the other person what specifically upset me, and I ask for what would work better for me. People are not mind readers. No one knows how I'm feeling or what I need *unless* I speak up.

Unfulfilled Expectation

My expectations are the impetus that drives me to act. If I do not expect to accomplish something, I don't bother pursuing it in the first place. Expectations become the bane of my existence when things don't turn out the way I want them to and when I don't get my way.

My expectations set the bar on how high I am willing to reach and on how far I am willing to go. At times, I have based my success on the fulfillment of my expectations. The problem with this lies in how I respond when faced with a setback.

Sometimes a setback throws me into a full blown three-year-old temper tantrum. I have also allowed unfulfilled expectations to cause me to give up on certain dreams.

My expectations significantly impact people and have a profound effect on how people show up for me. Of course, it works the other way too: other people's expectations of me have a significant impact on how I show up for them.

Helen Keller's gifts to the world would have remained hidden forever had her parents and Anne Sullivan not held high expectations of her.

Examples of unfulfilled expectations include:

- Wanting a promotion, but not getting it.
- Wanting a marriage to last forever, only to have it end in divorce.
- Wanting a child to earn straight A's in school, but he/she made a C in math.
- Expecting one's spouse to pick up a gallon of milk on their way home from work, only for them to forget the milk.
- Expecting a thank-you from one's spouse for cleaning out the garage, but not receiving it.
- Wanting a new computer for your birthday, but getting clothes instead.
- Wanting to make the soccer team, but not succeeding.
- Wanting the lead in the school play, but not getting it.
- Working out hard at the gym to lose five pounds this week, but gaining two instead.
- Wanting someone to change, and they won't.

Managing expectations is tricky. On the one hand, we very often get exactly what we expect to get. On the other hand, being upset over an unfulfilled expectation robs us of precious life energy.

Unfulfilled expectations are opportunities for me to stay open to the possibility that the thing I want may not be for my highest good, so something better is coming my way. They remind me to trust the process.

The more proficient I am in trusting that the very best thing for my highest good happened, or is happening, *even* when I don't understand how this is so, the better I feel.

Trust creates a space for me to achieve better results; the kind that make it more likely that my dreamsor something greater will come true. I say this because sometimes the universe conspires on our behalf, but we don't recognize this is what's happening in the moment.

To illustrate how the universe conspires on our behalf, here is a story I heard about a husband and wife traveling home from vacation:

> *Their flight was delayed for the second time. Jetlagged and grumpy, the wife approached the ticket agent at the counter. She demanded to know if there were any other flights available so that she and her husband could get home. The ticket agent politely told her that she was sorry, but there were no earlier flights available.*
>
> *The woman grew more frustrated. She was ready to be home. She was ready to sleep in her own bed. She was worried that she would miss seeing her son, a soldier, scheduled to return from Afghanistan for a brief layover back home.*
>
> *In a huff, she sat next to her husband in the gate area. He held out his cell phone to her and told her to read an email sent from their daughter. The email noted that their son's flight had been delayed. A couple of hours passed and the woman's frustration mounted. She felt like snapping when she noticed a group of soldiers coming down the ramp from another gate. She felt humbled. She was returning home from vacation; they were returning home from war.*
>
> *Her husband squeezed her arm as he pointed at the soldiers. He said, "Look." She told him that she saw them. He told*

her to look again. In an instant, her frustration over the delays evaporated. When she saw her son among the group of soldiers, she was thankful for the delay.

Whenever I'm faced with an unfulfilled expectation, I am learning to stay open to the possibility that something greater is coming my way.

Withholds or Undelivered Communications

Withholds, or undelivered communications, are comprised of the things I want to tell someone but have not.

Most often, communications are withheld or undelivered out of fear. We withhold what we want to say when we fear:

- The possible repercussions.
- Causing a scene.
- Not being liked.
- Losing our job, a relationship, or something we value.
- Hurting someone's feelings.

Sometimes communications are withheld because we believe it wouldn't make a difference or change anything anyway. At other times, communication is withheld because we do not want to deal with the other person's reaction. I've learned that both speaking out and not speaking out have consequences.

Sometimes the consequence is harmless. Sometimes the consequence is massive.

Not speaking out sooner lead to the killing of approximately six million Jews during the Holocaust.

Speaking out led to the creation of the Constitution of the United States of America.

Speaking out led to women getting the right to vote.

Speaking out led to the Civil Rights Movement.

Speaking out led to the Gay Rights Movement.

Not speaking out leads to bullies getting away with tyranny.

Sometimes, I am afraid of what might happen if I speak out. I'm still learning to speak out anyway. I'm learning that people are not fragile and that they hear what I say when I come from a place of love and concern for their well-being.

Likewise, people have told me things that stung, but I needed that stinging to wake up to a greater possibility than I saw for myself at the time.

While I encourage people to speak out, this does not mean I condone being verbally aggressive with someone, calling them names, or degrading them in any way. It means that it's important to say what's on your mind with as much compassion as you can muster at the moment.

If someone walks away and ends my relationship with them because of something I've said, at least I know I made the effort. I don't have to live with the dreaded *what if...* and *if only I had...*

When people leave my life, it's because we both have somewhere else to go. It's part of trusting the process:

> *I once met my neighbor while out walking my dogs. This neighbor was friendly enough, and I responded in kind. Shortly after meeting her, it became apparent to me that she was struggling. She was perpetually unhappy and seemed to be in a constant state of victimhood.*
>
> *Over a period of about a year, I offered her support. Nothing changed. She was famous for doing the "yes, but..." and offered many reasons why her life circumstances could not change.*

After being as compassionate as I knew how to be toward her, and after offering her ample support, I was over her chronic complaints and negativity. I changed my routine, walking the dogs at different times in hopes of avoiding her.

One day, I realized how I let her affect me. It was better for my schedule to walk my dogs when she often walked her dog. I mustered up my courage and opted to walk at that time of day.

Of course, I encountered her, and she started playing her poor me, victim song. She said, "I thought you were sick of me and were avoiding me." I'm sure she was not looking for the answer I gave her.

As gently as I knew how, I responded, "Well, now that you mention it… yes. I have been avoiding you." Before she got too far into the victim track she was playing, I let her know that I believed in her ability to have a happier life. I told her I saw tremendous potential in her. I told her that I was tired of her chronic negativity and complaining, and that's why I avoided her.

Some major drama followed on her part. She stormed off and made a point to avoid me after that. I was sad, but I'd given it my best shot. Eventually, she moved away and I lost track of her.

About 16 years later, I ran into a woman at a business gathering who looked familiar, but I couldn't place her. Our eyes met. She approached me. She asked me if I recognized her. I was honest, saying she looked familiar but I couldn't place her. She told me her name, and it clicked.

My former neighbor.

The transformation was tremendous. She looked fabulous! With a twinkle in her eye, she told me that she wasn't sure if she'd forgiven me yet, but that that moment on the sidewalk when I told her why I was avoiding her was a pivotal moment in her life.

She said once she had calmed down—about 10 years later— she had an epiphany. She admitted she was sick and tired of herself and went on to share that she realized it was time for her to give herself a good makeover.

What a makeover she had given herself! She seemed happy and looked positively stunning. We did not go on to become best friends, but I'm grateful she let me know how things turned out for her.

Each one of us has something significant to contribute. Every voice matters. Words have power. Words and action have an impact.

Speak up and speak out to say what's in your heart more than what's on your mind, and you'll discover what a force for greater good your words are.

What would make you feel better?

Acting on the answers to the questions in this chapter makes people feel better. In addition to the information you obtained by answering the above questions:

- What steps are you willing to take now to play to your own and other people's strengths?
- Are the key people in your life willing to be supported in addressing their weaknesses? If so, how might you support them?
- If not, I encourage you to focus on addressing your own weaknesses and leave them alone.
- What are you upset about?
- Are you willing to take courageous actions to address your upsets?

Chapter 4

The Fourth Courageous
Practice – Framing Things

The fourth courageous practice examines how to frame things so that you feel better and get better results. To help you frame things to your advantage, I'll share three techniques we use to make sense of our lives in a way that will get you out of the soup bowl and onto the balcony: definitions, models, and the debriefing technique.

Definitions

A definition acts as a lens which determines my experience of something. I see what the lens—or definition—allows me to see.

There may be a billion other viable definitions, but when I am *not* aware of the lens that I am looking through and its limitations, I cannot see the other viable possibilities.

In other words, my vision is narrowed and constricted.

For example, a general definition of health might be freedom from disease or injury.

Medical science may define health as the condition of an organism in which it performs its vital functions properly.

A general scientific definition of health might be the level of functional and metabolic efficiency of a living organism.

Health can also be defined in terms of life expectancy or longevity.

Notice each definition or lens shapes what I pay attention to when it comes to my health.

For instance, what happens if I ask myself: "Am I free from disease and injury?"

My answer may be yes, but I may not physically be able to do some of the things I enjoy doing (e.g., rock climbing, dancing, playing the violin, walking the dog). I could be 86-years-old, but mentally unable to do the things I want to do (e.g., balance my checkbook or recognize my family).

Is that healthy?

My definition of health includes more than how long I'll live, and it doesn't have a whisper of disease in it. It also doesn't focus on medical descriptors such as blood pressure, cholesterol, and blood glucose.

That doesn't mean I am ignoring those things. To me, health means more than the definitions used above. Definitions draw my attention toward specific information while excluding other information.

Where my attention goes, my creative energy flows. My creative energy flows in the direction of the lens I use to define health. In the above, more traditional definitions of health, one definition draws my attention toward disease.

When I remain focused on disease, my energy starts flowing in the disease direction.

Another definition draws my attention to my body as an organism. Viewing my body as an organism fails to account for the mental and spiritual aspects of my being.

By focusing solely on longevity, I could be 150-years-old and on life support but be considered healthy.

None of these definitions draw my attention in a direction that I want my creative energy flowing. That's why I created a definition of health that draws my creative energy in the direction I want to experience.

My Definition of Health

For me, health means I'm able to do the things I want to do and that I feel good when doing them. I have my wits about me. My intellect is sharp. I feel good in my body. I walk around with a spring in my step. I am happy. I feel vitally alive. I have a sense of purpose. I do good things in the world. I have fun. I enjoy life and I enjoy my body.

I exude vibrant, radiant, resplendent health. I am well able to do what I want to do. I laugh frequently. I am flexible, and I am strong. I am physically fit. I look good and feel good in my clothes. I feel connected to my Source. I'm optimistic about my future. I am constantly learning new things. I eat foods that nurture my body and support its optimal functioning. I am balanced.

My definition directs my focus and creative energy in the direction I want my health to go.

Does yours? Your definition directs how your creative energy flows.

Because I am clear on how I define health, I am the authority on my health. While I may consult with doctors and other healthcare practitioners, I know my body best because I am most in tune with it. I listen to and honor my body. I trust my Source to provide me with optimal health on a breath-by-breath basis.

When I consult with a doctor or other healthcare practitioner, I compare what they say with what my body and my spirit tell me, and I proceed from there. Sometimes that means disregarding what the professionals say; most often, it means combining their approach with what my body and spirit tell me is important.

Here are a couple of examples of how my definition of health led me to feel better and get better results:

Keeping my Dream of Being a Firefighter Alive in the Face of a Health Challenge

A few years into my firefighting career, I began experiencing an unusual amount of fatigue. Its onset was gradual, though constant. I experienced a lot of inexplicable muscle and joint pain, though no swelling or redness was evident. I also had bouts of sore throats, dizziness, nausea, and diarrhea that were out of the ordinary for me. At first, I thought I had the flu, but the symptoms persisted long after it would ordinarily take the flu to run its course.

Sleep did not relieve my extreme fatigue. As uncomfortable as this was, what disturbed me the most was how my body responded to exercise. I loved exercising. Running and lifting weights were a source of great pleasure for me, and my job as a firefighter depended on them. Activities that once left me feeling invigorated now made me feel much worse.

I took a short break from my training regimen. When this did not relieve this unusual fatigue, I went to the doctor. My doctor conducted a thorough physical examination which revealed that the lymph nodes in my neck and armpits were tender and enlarged. He also conducted some tests (e.g., blood tests and a urine test). After his exam was completed, my doctor diagnosed me with Chronic Fatigue Syndrome (CFS).

This was in the early 1990s, and not much was known about the condition. He told me that they did not know what caused the syndrome, nor did they know the best treatment for it. He also told me that the syndrome limits most people's ability to carry out ordinary daily activities. He told me I would need to restrict my social and recreational activities by limiting how much I exercised.

He went on to state that many people diagnosed with this condition ended up homebound and requiring help with daily activities such as getting dressed, eating, and bathing.

Throughout his discourse, I felt shell shocked. Minimal exercise? Limited recreational activities? When he said the word homebound something inside of me snapped. No! This is unacceptable! This is not my idea or definition of health! No way!

I interrupted him. "This doesn't work for me!" I stated firmly, clearly, and with complete authority. "I have too much to do to let this stop me!" I declared emphatically. The doctor was not pleased to be interrupted, nor was he pleased with what he perceived to be me disagreeing with his professional opinion. He was the doctor. He did his best to persuade me to listen to him and follow his advice.

I told him that while I appreciated his expertise, I had to find another way, a way that would allow me to continue to do the things I loved doing. He got angry and stormed out of the exam room. I left his office and got on with the business of discovering what worked best for my body and what would empower me to continue doing the things I loved to do.

In dealing with CFS, I stood up to the doctor and the prognosis he gave me, and I stood up to CFS itself. On mornings when I woke up feeling like I'd been hit by a runaway freight train, not feeling like getting out of bed, I did not cave into those feelings. Instead, I coached myself into action by reminding myself of how important it was for me to do the things I loved to do. I saw myself doing the things I love to do. I talked back to my disease. I talked back to my fear.

I faced CFS on my own terms. Having this condition advanced my ability to listen to and tune into what works for my body. When I listen to and honor my body and my spirit, I do well. As you listen to and tune into your body and spirit, you will do well too.

A Combined Approach and Alternative Methods Leads to Astounding Results

More recently, I experienced what I consider to be extraordinary results from working with a Traditional Chinese Medicine (TCM) Doctor.

For a few years, I suffered from pain, numbness, and tingling in my arms and hands at night when sleeping. I'd wake up several times to change positions in hope of falling back to sleep tingle- and pain-free.

In speaking with a medical doctor, he suggested that I might be suffering from ulnar nerve entrapment or some type of nerve damage from a neck and shoulder injury I experienced back in my firefighting days. The treatment course he recommended would have involved several expensive medical tests, anti-inflammatory medications, pain medications, and possible surgery. Intuitively, this approach did not feel right to me.

Instead of blindly following the doctor's recommendation, I turned inward. Over a period of two to three weeks, I meditated and asked my body what it needed to heal. I prayed. In meditation and prayer, my body sent me the clear message that I would benefit from Traditional Chinese Medicine, or more specifically, acupuncture.

While I had heard of acupuncture, I did not know much about it or Traditional Chinese Medicine. So before rushing off to find a practitioner, I conducted a little research. Acupuncture is an aspect of Traditional Chinese Medicine that has been practiced for twenty-three centuries. Chinese medicine operates on the premise that the body holds vital life energy called Qi or Chi, (pronounced "chee") which flows through pathways in the body called meridians.

Practitioners of TCM believe that illness occurs when one's Chi is blocked or unbalanced. Placement of acupuncture needles at various points along the meridians stimulates the body's natural healing abilities by triggering the release of healing chemicals and hormones like opioids and other peptides. Inserting the needles unblocks the dam in the river allowing one's Chi to reestablish its normal, healthy flow.

My research led me to a local TCM doctor who is a certified TCM practitioner, licensed acupuncturist, and licensed massage therapist with over fourteen years of experience.

I saw the TCM doctor in 2012, and I was amazed when she cured my symptoms in one visit through acupuncture. While having a bunch of needles inserted into one's body sounds about as soothing as wrestling naked with a porcupine, the actual treatment was relaxing. As the doctor inserted the thin, flexible needles in my body, I felt a slight pressure. It did not hurt.

In addition to acupuncture, the doctor gave me some Chinese herbs to help me get my sleep cycle back on track. The beautiful thing about the Chinese herbs was that they did not make me feel dopey the next day like the over-the-counter sleep aids I'd used in the past. The herbs the doctor gave me relaxed me. After I saw the TCM doctor that day, I had the best night's sleep I'd had in years. It's been more than four years since I saw her, and the pain and tingling in my arms and hands is still gone.

In the above stories, my definition of health put my focus and creative energy in the direction I wanted my health to go. Your definition directs how your creative energy flows.

How well do your definitions empower you to feel better and obtain optimal results in the following areas?

- Your overall sense of well-being.
- Your relationships.
- Your career.
- Your financial health and well-being.
- Your physical, emotional, and spiritual health.
- The things that interest you, excite you, ignite you, and that you are passionate about.

If you are in pain over not getting the results you want in any area of your life, it's time to look at how you define things. This gives you the ability to adjust your definitions so that your creative energy flows in a direction that produces optimal results.

Our definitions explain what we mean when we use certain words and form the basis for us being able to relate to and connect with one another. Without shared meaning, we would be lost.

Linked closely to definitions, is the second technique that plays an instrumental role in how to frame things to your advantage so you get out of the soup bowl of life and onto the balcony. I touched on this concept earlier. It's the concept of models.

Models

Earlier, I pointed out that if I were to give you an airplane model kit and ask you to assemble it, you would expect to create a replica of an airplane, not an orangutan. You noticed that you don't question that assembling an airplane model will result in a replica of an airplane. You are clear that you would not expect to create a replica of an orangutan from an airplane model kit.

We have models for most things in life, here are a few main ones:

- What it takes to feel good about ourselves.
- How to be a good friend/daughter/son/parent/spouse/employer/ employee.

- What it takes to obtain peace of mind.
- How to live our lives on purpose.
- What it takes to be financially solvent.
- How to succeed in our careers.
- What it takes to maintain a sense of well-being and to be satisfied with our lives.

While we have models for most things in life, to illustrate how important it is to know the parameters of a model, I will use the United States healthcare model for illustrative purposes. The U.S. healthcare model seems to go something like this when we get sick or injured:

- Go to doctor.
- The doctor investigates:
  - Conducts an examination.
  - Performs tests.
  - Prescribes/Conducts:
    - Medicationswhich come with long list of side effects which sound horrifying.
    - Treatments like radiation and chemotherapy.
    - Surgery.
- Patient gets better, or reapply model as outlined above.

People continue to operate within this healthcare model even though none of the prescription medications, treatments, or surgeries cures illnesses like heart disease, cancer, chronic lower respiratory disease, strokes, Alzheimer's disease, diabetes, kidney disease, or suicide.

People continue to seek out the magic pill to cure their ailments even though many prescription medications cause horrifying side effects and, in rare cases, death.

Albert Einstein said: *"Insanity is doing the same thing over and over again and expecting a different result."* To me, it seems reapplying the healthcare model described above and expecting a different result is insane.

I'm not convinced this model is the best healthcare model for me to apply so that I achieve and sustain optimal health. I wonder what we're missing? I wonder what the U.S. healthcare model is missing? What might your personal healthcare model be missing?

In my humble opinion, the U.S. healthcare model fails to account for the profound connection between my body, my mind, my emotions, and my spirit. In its failure to treat me as a multifaceted being, it also fails to hold me accountable for the actions and choices I have made/ am making that impact my health. It fails to ask me to take personal responsibility for my health and well-being.

The healthcare model has the doctors and nurses playing heroic rescuer and has me playing the role of victim to the big, bad cooties that may invade my body. Our culture rewards me for getting sick by letting me off the hook for certain things. Think about it, if you don't want to go to work which excuses would you give your boss:

a. I'm very sick, description of symptoms optional.
b. I don't want to come into the office today because I'm going water skiing at the lake (or engaging in some other fun activity).

I bet you picked option a) as the excuse for not going to work.

Why?

Because to a degree, our culture has space for people to call out sick. Our culture does not have space for us to tell the truth about our heart's desires without the possibility of facing what we perceive of as some dire consequences (e.g., getting fired, being ridiculed, or facing other people's anger/judgments).

Many people, healthcare practitioners included, fail to consider how not listening to and honoring our heart's desires, or our genuine interests. Our passions can then lead to us abusing our bodies with food, drugs, alcohol, and eating disorders.

Our healthcare model does not address the hefty price we pay because of our need to look good. We are so driven by our need to look good that it wreaks havoc on our bodies. Our fear over looking good causes us to:

- Work too many hours.
- Develop eating disorders or exercise excessively to be thin,
- Remain in unhappy/unhealthy relationships because we don't want to hurt anyone's feelings or get fired, or because we fear being alone.

Our healthcare model has us trudging into the doctor's office for a pill that we hope will cure us but fails to treat us as a whole person. It's important not to blame the doctors, the pharmaceutical companies, and the insurance companies for doing this to us.

We do it to *ourselves* because we have become a culture that seeks instant gratification.

We have failed to tune into the wisdom found in nature: that you must plant a seed in good soil for it to blossom. If the soil is not good in the first place, it must be amended and optimized so that it becomes good, fertile soil. Once the seed is planted in good soil, you must water it, weed it, fertilize it, and tend to it well so that it blossoms.

This is not an instantaneous process; there is a cycle and a rhythm to this process that unfolds over seasons.

As a multidimensional being, I owe it to myself and to others to learn from what nature offers me so that my being and my life blossoms (e.g., my career model, my relationship model, my financial model, my peace of mind model). This requires me to be mindful, and treat each area of my multidimensional being with tender, loving care.

Closely connected to the concept of models and how to grow the garden called you and your life is the third technique that frames things to your advantage and gets you out of the soup bowl and onto the balcony of life.

I call it debriefing.

Debriefing

Debriefing provides a strategic lens through which to look at each significant event that occurs, especially highly emotionally charged events. In the Fire Department, after each serious call we responded to, we would conduct a debriefing session.

The debriefing session took place in a no fault, learning environment. The goal was to improve our response because we knew a better response translated to saving more lives. In our debriefing sessions, each team member answered the following four questions:

1. What worked well?
2. What didn't work?
3. How will we capture what worked well so we repeat it?
4. How will we improve upon what didn't work so it will work better?

You may have heard this technique referred to as *lessons learned*. This approach allows you to improve individual and team performance in a non-judgmental, playing-for-results kind of way. It also acknowledges that we will do some things well while leaving room for the possibility for improvement.

What follows are three examples of how debriefing helped me feel better and get better results in my life.

Example 1 – Debriefing My Childhood

Situation:

Earlier, I shared how in my childhood layers of not enough and not good enough got caked onto my psyche. I shared how I felt like no matter what I did, I was not good enough, and how I came to believe that the world would be a better place without me in it.

Now I will apply the debriefing technique to this situation so that you see how it led me to feeling better about myself and my life.

What worked well:

What worked well for me as a child was my sense of adventure. I loved exploring new places, new trees, and new trails. I loved being outside and playing in nature. I loved riding my bike, reading, and using my imagination to create stories about a happier life. And, I loved to laugh.

What didn't work:

I felt suffocated. I felt overwhelmed by my parent's unhappiness with each other, and my inability to fix it. I felt hopeless from not being the child either of them wanted. Mom wanted a girly girl who loved pink, lace, and dresses. Dad wanted a rough and tumble son to take fishing, to teach how to repair things, and to do other manly stuff with. I felt worthless because the church condemned me to hell for being gay, one of the many traits I was born with.

Capturing what worked well so it will be repeated:

Being adventuresome outside and exploring nature works well for me. While I did not have the words for it at the time, nature connected me with the Powerful Presence of God. In nature, I experienced my Creator, God, as Pure Unjudging Love.

Playing in the woods, I awoke to the Presence of a Loving Creator who is and always has been for me. This experience serves me well, particularly when life throws me too many curveballs all at once. When I feel like the undertow of life is dragging me under, I know the moment has come to spend more time in nature. Out there in nature with God's Loving Presence, I am restored, fortified, and can tap into creative solutions for whatever challenges I face.

Improving upon what didn't work so it will work better moving forward:

When I spend too much time trying to please others instead of honoring my authentic self, I feel like I'm suffocating. When I am more invested in attempting to solve people's problems than they are, I feel the heavy weight of the ocean upon me. These feelings remind me that I'm off course.

To get back on course, I now understand that people want what they want from me, but that does not mean it's my job to give it to them. I now understand that it's best to be myself and follow the path that honors who I am rather than trying to live up to everyone else's expectations of me.

I also learned the importance of choosing one's spouse wisely. I learned that it's important to choose a spouse that I don't want to change; a spouse I love and appreciate exactly as they are.

I learned how important it is to be honest with myself about what I want in a spouse, and to be honest with potential suitors. I've noticed that vibrant relationships are created when I don't settle for less. I've also learned that happy relationships require me to focus on what's mine to give to the other person rather than focusing on what they can do for me. I also learned more about what does work from relationships that did not work.

Example 2 – The Work Project

Situation:

I had the opportunity to work on a project for an organization that I once thought would be my ideal employer. I loved the organization's mission, and I felt that I had something valuable to offer them given my professional background and career experience.

What I *didn't* know when I signed up for the project was that the lead on the project was a guy who doesn't listen. This guy did not listen to us, his team, or to our client. He had a bad habit of stepping over what our client attempted to say in meetings.

It was stressful to watch our client's body tense up to the brink of exploding whenever the project lead cut him off. It was so bad we thought the client might fire us. Not long into the project, it became apparent that this guy thought his way was the best way to approach and do everything.

A-ha! Lightbulb moment!

That's why the project lead didn't think he needed to listen to anyone else. This poor guy saw asking questions and listening as a weakness or liability, rather than an asset and strength.

What worked well?

The team pulled together to learn what we needed to know to satisfy our client when the project lead was not around. The team fed information back to the project lead so that we had the information needed to keep the project on track. This enabled us to keep our client relatively happy.

What didn't work?

Having a leader who does not listen caused morale on our team to plummet, and damn near cost us our jobs. People on our team did not want to be there. Our team could have delivered much better products to our client had the project lead listened to the client's needs.

No matter how good our team was at feeding client information back to the project lead, some things got lost in translation. Our team would have delivered far better products had the project lead been receptive to the team's input on how to approach the project, on how to complete tasks, and on what products and services would be most beneficial to our client.

How will we capture what worked well so we repeat it?

What worked well was the team deftly figuring out how to connect with the client and finding ways to keep the client satisfied. What worked well was the team setting aside their egos in favor of the good of the overall project. What worked well was attempting to address the project lead's failure to listen to him directly even though–guess what–he did not listen.

At least we know we attempted to address his behavior. What also worked well was the team connecting with the client, asking the client questions and delivering what the client asked for—despite pushback from the project lead.

How will we improve upon what didn't work so it will work better?

The biggest lesson for me from this project is an expanded awareness of what kinds of projects and people I'm willing to take on, as well as what kinds of projects and people I'm not interested in working with.

I got that I want to work with people who are creating great things in the world. Doing this requires listening: both listening to myself and listening to the people involved on the project, whether I agree with what they say or not.

I also learned that once our attempt to address the project lead's behavior was unsuccessful, it would have served me much better to resign and move on to the next best thing.

Example 3 – The Dating Scene

Situation:

If you've ever been on the dating scene, you may have had experiences like mine. I would often show up on a first date to discover one of two things: a) that I had been lied to or b), that I was being walked down the aisle in holy matrimony without knowing the other person and without her knowing me.

And, yes… I'm talking about the very first date.

My friends and I talked about this, and many of them encountered these same two scenarios on their first dates. It was as if the other person did not believe me when I said, "non-smoking." They magically thought that even though I said athletic, I'd settle being saddled with a couch potato for the rest of my life.

Even more distressing were the women I met for the very first time who instantly saw us married and living happily ever after. This one was particularly off putting to me because I want to get to know someone before making a life-long commitment, and I want them to get to know me too.

What worked well?

What worked well when I was on the dating scene was putting myself out there, which increased my chances of finding what I wanted. I did not stay home, sitting on the sidelines, hoping I'd meet someone someday.

What didn't work?

I'm not sure if it was other people's wishful thinking I bumped up against, or if I somehow failed to communicate effectively. Whatever it was showing up and having someone not be who they presented themselves as did not work for me. Having women who did not know me want to marry me seemed flat out foolish to me.

How will we capture what worked well so we repeat it?

Now that I'm happily married, it's hard to imagine ever needing to repeat what worked. If I had to, I'd say it's putting myself out there and being honest and forthright about who I am, what I'm up to in the world and what I'm looking for.

What also worked well was that I refused to settle.

When I showed up, having made it clear that I wanted a non-smoker, and met someone smoking at the bar, I knew this person was not suitable dating material for me. It did not matter when she said, "but I only smoke when I'm drinking or on the weekends hanging out with my friends at the lake."

When I said non-smoking, I meant it, and honoring that worked for me. I also knew when someone had us walking down the aisle of holy matrimony before getting to know me that I was best served by running fast and far in the other direction.

I don't need that kind of heavy desperation in my life!

How will we improve upon what didn't work so it will work better?

After trying the online dating scene, I decided to stop going down that track. It seemed too easy for people to misrepresent themselves online.

I decided to focus on doing the things I enjoyed doing and trust that when the time was right, the right one would show up.

That's exactly what happened.

I met my beautiful spouse at a pool party, where we were playing and having fun with many other friends. We took our time in getting to know each other, learning each other's strengths and weaknesses. We learned that we work well together as a team and that what we create together is beautiful.

Applying the Debriefing Technique to Your Life

How will you implement the debriefing technique to effect positive results in your health, relationships, and/orfinances? How will you use it in your career? In your company/business/church?In your hobbies?In the other important areas of your life?

What would make you feel better?

In addition to answering the above questions:

- How well are your definitions serving you?
- Are you missing vital information because of what your definitions screen out?

- If where your attention goes, your creative energy flows, are you creating the results you want in each area of your life?
- If not, what definitions need adjusting?
- How well are your models working for you?
- Are you subscribing to any models that have you repeating the same steps and/or taking the same actions but expecting a different result?
- If so, how might you expand the model so you get better results?
- What new and different actions might you need to take?
- How well are you listening to and honoring your genuine interests and passions?
- Are you numbing out by overindulging in food, drugs, alcohol, or starving yourself?
- Are you working too many hours, exercising excessively, remaining in any unhappy/unhealthy relationships?
- If so, are you willing to address these areas so that you can feel better and get better results?
- Are you willing to release your need for instant gratification and work with the natural cycle and rhythm of the Creative Process to create a life that works for you even if it takes a few seasons?
- Are you willing to implement the Debriefing Technique on an ongoing basis so that you are empowered to learn what you need to learn to feel better and get better results on a continual basis?

A Special Bonus from Denise

Now that you have your copy of *Made to Thrive: Eight Courageous Practices to Improve Your Life, Find Inner Peace and Be Happy*, you are on your way to:

- Feeling better about yourself (i.e., who you are and how you interact with others)
- Feeling optimistic about your opportunities and possibilities
- Getting better results in your relationships, at work and at play

Plus...you'll soon find yourself experiencing more peace and happiness.

You'll also receive the special bonus journal I created to add to your toolkit. The journal gives you a central place to capture your responses to the questions contained inside. You may want to refer back to your answers as you grow and expand, or face different challenges moving forward.

There's so much confusing information out there about how to improve your life, find inner peace and happiness. When you finish this book, you'll be armed with eight courageous practices that will help you feel better and get better results.

While this journal is offered for sale, as a special bonus you can claim it for free here:

www.denisegarrett.com/bookbonus.

I believe you were made to thrive.

I'm in your corner. Let me know if I can help further.

Here's to you creating a life where you positively thrive!

Best,
Denise Garrett

Chapter 5

The Fifth Courageous
Practice – Service and Vision

The fifth courageous practice is what I call being in service to your highest vision.

Being of Service

What is your reason for waking up every morning, getting up out of bed, and proceeding with the tasks at hand for the day? What *really* matters to you in your life? What do you love, and what energizes you?

These questions can be used to describe or develop our sense of purpose and to help us realize how we will use our unique gifts, talents, and interests in the service of others.

I feel the greatest sense of fulfillment when I step outside of myself (e.g., my own issues, concerns, and struggles) and step into the world of another. The more I aim to be of service to others and to make a positive difference in the life of someone else, the better I feel.

Being of service to others motivates me to get out of bed on those days when I don't feel well, or when I wake up feeling bone-deep tired.

As I shared earlier when I was diagnosed with Chronic Fatigue Syndrome, my desire to continue serving as a firefighter kept me going. What keeps me going to this day is my sense of purpose.

I also credit my desire to serve with helping me get over my deep-seated sense of worthlessness. The more I focus on being of service, the more I quiet the old, self-defeating "not enough" tune that used to play incessantly in my head.

What's Mine to Give

Even when I'm in my deepest angst and despair struggling with my issues about not being enough, not belonging, or feeling worthless, I've noticed that by asking myself one simple question, I am transported to a much better place.

The question is:

What is mine to give? What is mine to give right now, in this moment, to this person or group of people?

As I focus my energy on giving what is mine to give, I am transported to a better place, and I become a person who makes a positive difference.

While camping in September of 2015, I had an epiphany.

I discovered the subtle, but powerful, difference between what it means to attempt to change something or someone, versus focusing on what is mine to give to a cause or to a person.

Change meets with resistance. Imagine attempting to change the direction a river flows in. You would never try to do that because you would be the one who got washed downstream.

The river is too powerful.

Organizations are full of well-meaning people who want to change things. Many people set out to change the world, but what usually happens when someone introduces change into a relationship or organization is people resist their attempts to change things.

Attempting to change things is like driving a Maserati at full speed into a solid concrete wall and expecting the wall to move out of the way before impact occurs. That's why the saying *the only thing you can change is yourself* rings true.

Change requires willingness and desire on the part of an individual or an entire group of people.

History has shown us that when enough like-minded and like-hearted people come together for a common cause, change happens. Like a lot of other people, I see things in the world that I want to be different (e.g., elimination of discrimination in all its forms, an end to hunger and poverty, no more violence and war, people to stop using tobacco products, and no more fear).

Yet I've experienced how powerless I feel to change everything, and everyone I'd like to change.

While camping on this one trip, I saw the subtle, yet powerful, difference between focusing on what I want to change versus focusing on what's mine to give.

For years, I wanted to change my mother's worrywart ways. I felt suffocated by her attempts to keep me from doing things I wanted to do because of her fear for my safety.

I realized she was trying to be a good mom, and our paradigm of a good mom is a mom who is concerned for their child's well-being and safety.

My understanding of this did not stop me from feeling suffocated when she would voice her fears over whatever activity I was pursuing. I got angry and upset.

I'm pretty sure that I upset her as well.

Then, the question popped into my head: What is mine to give? Remember, I can't change my mom, but I can figure out what's mine to give her.

I am still going to do things that cause my mom to fear for my safety and well-being. Not because I'm malicious, but because I am a different person than she is. I am more comfortable taking certain kinds of risks than she is.

What I can do is a better job of ensuring her of all the safety measures I've taken when I tell her about the activity I am going to do. I can do my best to give her comfort while still doing my own thing.

Of course, sometimes this means not sharing things with my mom until after I've already done them so I can show her all is well.

In some situations, the best I can give is my refusal to participate. For example, when I encounter a group of people who are caught up in how awful things are, I can best serve everyone by refusing to participate.

If the group I encountered is going on about how bad the economy is, I may stand among them silently affirming that I am grateful that I always have plenty, that God is my Source and God is Infinite; therefore, my very nature is that of abundance and opulence.

On other occasions, I might slip quietly away from the group and get back to work.

Overall, I've learned that when I ask myself what is mine to give, I am steered in a different direction than the one I would pursue if I attempt to change someone.

Focusing on giving steers me in a direction that creates a generosity of spirit within me that produces significantly better results. When people offer us a gift, we accept it or decline it; we don't resist it.

The next time you meet someone you want to change, ask yourself: What's mine to give? Notice, the person will either accept your offering, or they will decline it. As you come from the generous space of offering what is yours to give, you will find people ready to receive the gift you are offering.

You will likely encounter some people who are not ready to receive what you offer them. When this happens, let go and choose to invest your precious life energy into giving what's yours to give to those open to receiving it.

By steadfastly focusing on the people who are open to receiving what is ours to give, we will eventually develop the critical mass needed to shift things in a direction that is in alignment with our highest vision of what we'd like to see different.

By focusing on what's yours to give in service to your highest vision, you align yourself with the divine creative flow of the universe so that magic and miracles have an avenue to show up.

Your Highest Vision

What's your highest vision? It's the image that comes to mind when I ask you two questions.

First question: How are you being and what are you doing when you are at your highest and best?

Examples of *being* may include:

- Being at peace.
- Laughing with your spouse or kids.
- Trusting that things are going to work out for the best.
- Having a healthy work-life balance.
- Being emotionally and/or physically balanced.
- Being vibrantly healthy.
- Being grateful for your many blessings.
- Being confident, kind, respectful, self-aware, optimistic, focused, and/or decisive.
- Being a person of your word.
- Inspiring and/or inspired.
- Remaining unflappable in the face of a crisis.

Examples of *doing* may include:

- Playing the violin.

- Painting.
- Performing on stage.
- Creating a great company.
- Giving food or medical supplies to poverty stricken people.
- Having plenty of money in the bank.
- Leading a church, business, organization, town, county, or country.
- Making other people laugh.
- Raising people's awareness.

Second question: What do you want to see changed in the world? For example, you may want to see a world:

- Full of healthy people.
- Where everyone has plenty of food and safe drinking water.
- Without violence and hate.
- Without discrimination and other –isms.
- Of equal opportunity and equal pay.
- Where people spend more time with their families and loved ones.
- With clean wholesome living space for everyone.
- Where everyone can read.
- That reveres forests and wildlife.
- In which everyone thrives.

These are only some examples. What image comes to your mind when I ask you how are you being and what are you doing when you are at your highest and best?

What do *you* want to see changed in the world?

Once you have your preliminary answers to these questions, you are in a good position to explore how to implement the fifth courageous practice: being in service to your highest vision.

Your answers shine a light on what traits you already have that set you up to feel good about you and your life path. Your answers also show you areas that you need to develop in yourself, skills you may want to master, who you can seek out to develop those traits and/or who can teach you those skills.

Of course, don't overthink it. When I wanted to be a firefighter, the one thing I knew for sure was that I needed to develop my physical strength. My passion, desire, and commitment to that vision carried me the rest of the way.

The good news is, you don't have to have it figured out before deciding to sink yourself into being the highest vision of yourself imaginable. You don't have to know how to change what you want to see changed in your world before getting started.

As you focus on the *what* and get in motion, what you need will show up.

I was and still am a firefighter at heart. I reached a place where something in me knew that to achieve the highest vision of myself possible and to create the thing I most wanted to create in the world, I had to let go of firefighting to become something greater.

That's why the universe closed the door on me staying in the fire service when I went to graduate school. That's why so many other wonderful opportunities opened for me when I decided to go to graduate school.

Each door that opened led me closer to my highest vision of myself, to being the change I want to see in the world. Each door opened new possibilities for how I engage with the world to effect the changes I want to see.

Notice I added being the change I want to see in the world. I've learned that for something to happen in my world, I must embody it first. It's an inside-out job versus an outside job.

The better I am at living the highest vision of myself possible, the more I see that happening in the people around me. While this may sound woo-woo to some folks, let me introduce a concept that will clarify any lingering doubts.

> **Question:** What is something that the more you give it away, the more of it you get?
>
> **Answer:** Love.

I've learned that love is the greatest factor that contributes to my ability to feel better and get better results.

Love

The times I've felt the best and achieved the best results are the times when:

- I focus on what I must give to someone else that will improve their situation.
- I am absorbed in doing the things I love to do (e.g., hiking, enjoying nature, writing, coaching).
- Someone loves me for me—warts and all,
- I choose love over fear.

For me, this is sometimes harder than it might sound because I bump up against my automatic defaults called:

- What will people think of me?
- What's in it for me?

When I'm in either mode, I'm coming from a place of fear. Fear is the antithesis of love. The challenge I face each day is recognizing when I'm scared. Failure to recognize that I'm afraid prevents me from having a choice.

Choice equals freedom. Fear equals slavery.

Fear cannot occupy the same space as love. They are magnetically opposing forces. Each is powerful and each can draw me in. However, one enslaves me while the other sets me free.

When I am conscious and aware that I'm in a fearful state, I have the power to choose love over fear.

When I chose love, magic happens.

When I let fear get the best of me, I lose and so do the people around me.

In contrast to sneaky fear, when I chose love, I trust that my needs are being met and will continue to be met, even though I might now know how. When I choose love, I am free and it sets me on course to feel better and obtain better results.

Choosing love doesn't mean that I sit back idly waiting to see what love will bring my way. Rather, it means that I choose to love myself enough to take good care of me. Choosing love means that I conscientiously pursue the things I love and express love to the best of my ability in any situation.

It may mean letting go of the *what's in it for me* and tuning into *what I have to give to someone* that will improve their situation. The more I practice this, the better I feel and the better my life gets.

It's no surprise that for me to feel better and get better results, I need to become more masterful at loving. To become more masterful at loving, it's important to clarify what I mean when I say the word, "love."

For instance, when I say the word, "Father," what comes up for you? Do you see an image of your dad or do you see the image of a priest?

Words have connotations that go far beyond the word itself. Whole worlds of meaning may be contained in any single word we speak. Given this, what does it mean when I say, I love you?

Rather than attempting to define something as vast and full of meaning as love, I've opted to defer to several descriptions of love that illustrate what I mean when I use the word.

For starters, I'll turn to what a group of 4 to 8-year-olds said when asked: What does love mean?

- "When my grandmother got arthritis, she couldn't bend over and paint her toenails anymore. So, my grandfather does it for her all the time, even when his hands got arthritis too. That's love." Rebecca - age 8.
- "When someone loves you, the way they say your name is different. You just know that your name is safe in their mouth." Billy - age 4.
- "Love is what's in the room with you at Christmas if you stop opening presents and listen." Bobby - age 7.
- "Love is when you tell a guy you like his shirt, and then he wears it every day." Noelle - age 7.
- "Love is like a little old woman and a little old man who are still friends even after they know each other so well." Tommy - age 6.
- "Love is when your puppy licks your face even after you left him alone all day." Mary Ann - age 4.

Another excellent description of what I mean when I use the word, love, came from author and motivational speaker, Leo Buscaglia, also known as "Dr. Love."

Mr. Buscaglia talked about a contest he was asked to judge. The purpose of the contest was to find the most caring child. The winner was a 4-year-old child whose elderly next-door neighbor recently lost his wife. Upon seeing the man cry, the little boy went into the old gentleman's yard, climbed onto his lap, and sat there. When his mother asked what he had said to the neighbor, the little boy said, "Nothing, I just helped him cry."

Love is using your power and influence to improve the quality of someone else's life. Love is a choice, not just a feeling. Love is a verb, an action, even when that action is holding a prayerful space for someone that their situation will improve. Love is the conscious embodiment of abundance and plenty.

The Stuff Miracles Are Made Of:

Love has a way of producing miraculous results. For example:

In October 2013, the entire Olivet Middle School football team went behind their coaches back. They schemed and conspired to plan a remarkable play. Their remarkable play: not scoring.

What motivated them to concoct this secret play? The team invented the secret play because they wanted to make someone happy, to make one particular someone's day.

Their plan involved getting as close to the goal line as possible without scoring so that Keith Orr, a kid with a learning disability, would have a chance to score a touchdown. At the one-yard line, one of the players took a dive even though he was wide open.

The crowd jeered with dismay until Orr took the field and scored the touchdown. The players wanted to show Orr that he meant a lot to them and to give him the joy that comes from scoring a touchdown. It took a minute for the fans to realize Orr scored because the team surrounded him, protecting him in the middle of the rush to the goal line.

The football team also gave Orr the gift of being cool because when the football team decides that you are cool, pretty much everyone follows suit.

Orr was not the only one who received a gift that day. One teammate shared that while the idea of letting Orr score wasn't his, he received a bigger gift from that secret play.

He went from being somebody who cared about himself
and his friends to caring about his community and trying to
make more peoples day better.

Olivet Middle School's football team affected more than their team that day. When the parents of Keith Orr realized that their son scored a touchdown, they found peace in knowing that the team was looking out for their son. The crowd was changed too as their jeers of dismay turned into cheers of inexplicable joy.

One act of loving kindness affected a whole stadium of people that day. Imagine what our world would look like if each one of us displayed loving kindness to as many people as we could each day.

Did you notice in the story above that the football players were not afraid of the crowd's jeers? The football players set out to make one boy's day, and in the end, they ended up making the crowd's day a bit brighter.

Each time we turn our attention away from fear and focus our energy and efforts on making love a verb, we win. It's a choice each one of us gets to make. Which will you choose: sneaky fear or love?

I say you have it in you to choose love, moment by precious moment.

What would make you feel better?

- Are you willing to live a service-driven life?
- What changes might you need to make to live a life of service?
- Think about someone or something you would like to see changed. Build your case as to *why* you think that person or situation needs changing. Imagine attempting to change the person or the situation by giving them the long list of why you think they need to change. How well do you imagine that conversation going?
- Now, instead of focusing on changing them, ask yourself what is yours to give them? Remember change meets with resistance, so when you encounter resistance, pause and ask yourself: What's mine to give?

- How are you being when you are at your highest and best (e.g., patient, generous, inspiring, optimistic, funny, playful, courageous, bold, honest)?

- What are you doing when you are at your highest and best (e.g., teaching children, running your own company, or leading the division of a company, performing onstage, making people feel better about themselves by cutting and styling their hair, making jewelry)?

- What do you want to see changed in the world?

- What do you have to give toward making that change happen?

- What do you have to give that will improve someone's situation?

- What are you doing when you lose track of time (e.g., leading a board meeting, keeping your company's books, writing an article/report/book/technical manual, investigating for a story, or to solve a crime)?

- Who loves you perceived flaws and all? (Hint: If you answered no one, start by loving and appreciating you and what you've been through).

- How proficient are you at courageously choosing to love over your fear? (Hint: I guarantee you that we have room for improvement here).

- How will you manage your automatic *what will people think of me* and *what's in it for me* so that you are present for others?

- What steps will you take to become more masterful at loving?

- What actions will you take daily to make love a verb?

- How will you use your power and influence to improve the quality of your own and someone else's life today?

- How will you be more loving toward yourself? Toward others?

- Are there people in your life to whom you need to express your appreciation?

- What changes do you need to make so that you strengthen your love and faith muscles to better defend yourself from fear?

Chapter 6

The Sixth Courageous Practice – You Gotta Have Faith

The sixth courageous practice involves developing your faith muscles. I'm talking about giving them a super good workout daily—especially on days when things are *not* going your way. When I talk about faith, I'm talking about relying more on your inner vision or imagination than you rely on your eyes, or what you see in your world right this moment.

Your Senses Point to a Greater Possibility

Pause and look at your surroundings.

What do you see?

A desk, a book, a mess that needs cleaning up, a chair, a candle burning?

What do you hear?

Music, your children playing in the background, an airplane flying overhead, office chatter, a telephone ringing?

What do you smell?

Fresh mown grass, flowers, bleach or disinfectant, grease, a campfire, dinner cooking?

What do you feel?

The softness of your clothing, the firmness of your bed, the coolness, or warmth of your HVAC?

What do you taste?

Refreshingly cool water, pizza, minty fresh breath, your favorite coffee, or tea?

The things you experience with your five senses came from someone's imagination. Each and every thing you sense started out as an idea that someone faithfully acted upon until they made visible what started from the invisible realm of their imagination.

The Power Inside of You

Think of something you've accomplished that you are proud of. It doesn't have to be something that anyone else noticed or anything on a grand scale. It just needs to be something that you are proud of yourself for doing. How did you accomplish it?

Perhaps you had an idea. It was something that you were excited about which motivated you to act. For you to have accomplished the thing that you are proud of, you also had to have faith. You had to have faith in the possibility that your idea would work and faith in your ability to accomplish it.

I've noticed that even the best ideas crash and burn when we lack faith in the possibility for change. When we don't have faith that something different can occur, one of two things happen:

- Nothing.
- We get more of the same old, same old thing.

I've also noticed that when great ideas are met with unwavering faith, faith in the possibility that we make a difference, here's what happens: a), inspiration that leads to b), inspired action or inaction, which leads to c), unprecedented results.

You might say, "Well, Denise, it's *far* easier to create a chair than it is to create global peace!" and that is a valid observation. The key takeaway here is understanding that what we experience started in someone's imagination.

Violence starts in one's imagination and so does peace. Poverty and scarcity start in one's imagination as does abundance and plenty. Both imaginings result in different actions which produce different outcomes.

Most firefighters I know are adept at leveraging their faith toward positive outcomes under some of the most difficult circumstances we humans experience. I know firsthand the power of staying calm, confident, and faith-filled in the face of fear. People involved in an accident or experiencing an emergency fare far better when the first responder stays calm and assures them that they are going to be okay.

Toddlers and children are the same way too. Toddlers and children turn to their caregivers to see how to react when they get hurt or sick. The results of such encounters would be different if the first responder or caregiver ran around, screaming about doom and gloom.

To illustrate how much impact remaining faith-filled under dire circumstances leads to miraculous results, I'll share the story about a woman who was trapped in her vehicle for nearly three hours in a horrific multi-vehicle accident.

Station Wagon Meets Tractor Trailer

I once worked on a lady who was trapped in her vehicle for almost three hours before being extricated and transported to the nearest medical facility.

The long and short of this incident is that a tractor-trailer attempted to make a U-turn on a two-lane road in the dark. As the tractor-trailer driver attempted to make the turn, the flatbed trailer portion carrying a steel I-beam was not visible to oncoming traffic.

A lady driving a station wagon behind him did not see him.

She slammed into the flatbed of the trailer. A domino effect occurred as vehicle after vehicle piled into the back of the vehicle in front of them, each one jamming the woman in the station wagon further under the flatbed trailer.

Many of the occupants from other vehicles were seriously injured and required extrication by the Fire Department. We fought hard against the golden hour in emergency medicine.

Because the station wagon was jammed so far underneath the tractor-trailer, we could not extricate the woman from her vehicle until a special crane arrived on scene.

As multiple rescue operations took place around us, I squeezed into the rear of the woman's station wagon to render aid.

Why me?

Because I was small enough to squeeze into the tiny space that used to be her back seat and cargo area.

Once I squeezed in, I assisted paramedics with starting IVs on her, holding C-spine on her, and checking her vital signs. I also assured her we were doing everything we could to get her out and that she would be okay.

The woman in the station wagon kept slipping in and out of consciousness. Regardless, I kept offering her what I hoped were comforting and reassuring messages like: "We're going to get you out of here. Hang in there with me. Think about your kids and your family who love you. You're going to be okay." I did not know if the woman heard me, but I kept sending her words of comfort and assurance.

I also, silently, prayed for her.

She had been unconscious for over an hour by the time we extracted her from her vehicle. It took almost three hours before we loaded her into the ambulance for transport to the hospital, but she was alive.

Flash forward, several months later.

A gentleman brought a lady in a wheelchair to visit our Station one day. The guys on shift that day told our shift that the woman wanted to thank the firefighters and paramedics who saved her life in person. She was the woman from the tractor-trailer accident.

She told them that she was very happy to be alive even though the road to recovery was painful. She told them that she kept feeling strong, reaffirming hands on her and hearing an encouraging voice that night that wouldn't let her give up regardless of her pain and no matter how scared she was.

Note that this is what First Responders do. They loan their strength and offer assurance to people in danger. The calming presence and concerted efforts of each rescue worker who responded to this call saved this woman's life.

If fear had won, chances are incredibly high that this woman would have perished.

Faith is the Optimizer

Faith affects me as an individual and the people around me. While fear pollutes our lives, faith optimizes us so that we are like a good, fertile soil that the seeds of our service and vision need to thrive and to blossom. Faith uproots the weeds of fear and doubt, creating optimal conditions for us to feel better and get the results we want.

Having faith in my dreams and my fellow humans does not mean that I always get what I want, or that what I want will be handed to me on a silver platter. I've learned that sometimes I'm better off *not* getting the exact thing I wanted. In my experience, not getting what I wanted has led to me receiving something far greater than what my limited soup bowl view of life imagined.

Faith is transcendent. How do I know this?

Because if I don't believe in the possibility of something, I don't pursue it and you won't either. In the absence of belief, dreams die snuffed out by a mistaken conviction that it's not possible. With faith, I can move mountains and obstacles become minor speed bumps I encounter along the road to fulfilling my dreams.

Faith turns obstacles into opportunities while fanning the flames of my heart so that I take inspired action. It compels me to keep going until I see what I set out to see. My conviction in my belief means I put more stock in my inner vision, or my imagination than I do in my outer worldly vision (e.g., news reports, or doctor's test results).

Faith demands that I act. While I might prefer quietly meditating on that which I desire and chanting affirmations hoping to attract what I want toward me, this approach does not guarantee my success. Meditation and affirmations merely set the stage for my success, but they do not secure it. To secure success, I must engage with the world and with the people around me.

Faith doesn't care about my comfort. In fact, it involves stepping outside my comfort zone. Ultimately, my belief means I care more about my dream than I do about whether other people ridicule me and that I am more committed to my vision or dream than I am to my comfort.

Most of us have had the experience of doing something uncomfortable. While it is unpleasant to change a baby's stinky diaper, we allow our nostrils to experience the temporary discomfort of the stinky diaper to show we care about the baby's well-being.

People who practice their music, dance, sport, or another area of interest also know what it means to experience temporary discomfort to experience a greater reward later.

Firefighters and other First Responders are familiar with letting go of their comfort to accomplish their goal, saving lives. In my own experience, I've noticed that when I choose to exercise my faith muscles and that I am willing to experience discomfort, amazing things happen which my logical mind cannot explain.

Faith taps into the power of intuition. This is a profound sense of knowing what I need to do, even though it might not make sense to anyone else or even seem illogical.

In my experience, acting on intuitive nudges has paid huge dividends. Honoring my intuition has produced excellent results; results which make me feel better.

Strengthening Your Faith Muscles

Building my faith muscles requires me to ensure that I am good soil and that I am a good gardener. This means I tend to my garden by:

- Cultivating the soil which is me.
- Planting the seeds that I want to see or experience.
- Weeding.
- Watering and fertilizing.
- Pruning.
- Being patient.
- Trusting the process.

Cultivating the Soil Which Is Me

It's easy to get caught up in the soup of other people's beliefs about what is possible and what isn't possible. When I don't like what I see on the outside, it's time to start examining what's happening with me on the inside.

- What do I believe?
- What are my judgments and how well do they serve me?
- What would I rather see?
- What new beliefs may I need to cultivate which offers more support to that which I would rather see?
- What judgments might I need to release so that my energy is not bogged down in negativity?

- Who can teach me, coach me, or mentor me?
- What actions am I taking on a consistent basis to create more of what I'd rather see?

Planting the Seeds That I Want to See/Experience

Earlier I asked you what image comes to your mind when you are at your highest and best. I asked what do you see yourself doing when you are at your highest and best, and I asked what you want to see changed in the world.

These are the seeds you must plant and nurture in the garden called your life. Now is the time to take personal responsibility for strengthening your faith muscles by doing whatever you can do toward that which you would rather be, see, and experience.

Weeding

Weeding means I remove any damaging influences that crop up. I weed out the things that steal energy from me being at my best. I cut out the stuff that steals energy from my vision of what I want to see and experience in my world. I can be the most positive person in the world with the grandest vision ever, but I won't remain that way if I don't remove the weeds that suck vital life energy away from me.

Some common weeds that need to be addressed so that we feel better and get better results include:

- Fear and its derivatives (e.g., doubt, worry, concern, angst, anxiety, and apprehension).
- Disempowering and limiting thoughts (e.g., it can't be done, not having what it takes, nothing ever changes).
- Limiting judgments and beliefs (e.g., I'm not good enough, I don't have what it takes to pursue my vision/mission/dreams, what I'm out to achieve is impossible, I'm too young, too old, too inexperienced, thoughts that diminish the people I encounter along life's way).

- The drama story and my participation in it (e.g., victim-rescuer-persecutor)
- Insisting that I'm right, thereby making others bad and wrong, or that I'm bad or wrong, thereby making someone else right.
- Naysayers, nonbelievers, negative Nellies, and chronic complainers.
- Habits that interfere with our progress toward our vision (e.g., overindulging in food, television, the internet, video games, texting, social media, partying, alcohol, tobacco and other drugs, not getting enough sleep, not getting enough exercise, and overspending).

Tossing aside judgments and beliefs that are hurtful, destructive, and limiting is one of the greatest acts of love known to humankind.

Developing habits that inspire and support us in being our best is also one of the greatest acts of love known to humankind.

This kind of love requires great courage and tremendous faith. Courage, faith, and love are the stuff giants are made of.

You have this giant power within you!

Giants are extremely adept at playing for their goals and dreams. With scalpel-like precision, they remove things that interfere with their progress. These exemplary people accept that they are a work in progress. Giants achieve amazing results by directing their eagle eyes toward weeding out their own impediments; as they weed out their own impediments, these courageous, faith-filled, and loving folks evaluate what else impedes their progress, and eliminate those people and habits accordingly.

Many people find it difficult to weed out the people in their life that bring out the worst in them, impeding their progress. Deciding to cut people out of one's life is a big decision, and sometimes a scary one. Fear creeps in.

What will people think about me if I abandon my sister in her time of need?

What if I end up needing something from this person down the road?

What if this relationship is as good as it gets?

What if I'm wrong about this person?

If you are not in the place to remove the hooks negative people have in you, I recommend you do your best to limit the amount of contact you have with them. By limiting your exposure to them, you limit a number of toxins they release your way.

Before you have contact with them, use some of the tools recommended in the watering and fertilizing segment below to inoculate yourself from them. As soon as possible after being around them, immerse yourself in the positive practices you've developed that feed, nourish, and inspire your soul.

Watering and Fertilizing

If you plant a seed in fertile soil but fail to water it and fertilize it, your plant will perish. To yield a thriving bumper crop in the garden of our lives, watering and fertilizing our faith is imperative. Water and fertilizer are the tools and techniques you implement to get out of the soup bowl of life and onto the balcony.

Some of the tools I've used to keep me on the faith-filled track include the following:

- Meditation.
- Put positive affirmations in places that I see throughout the day.
- Write my desire(s) on an index card that I carry with me and refer to throughout the day.
- Spend time with, watching, and listening to people who inspire me.
- Create a vision board and view it on a regular basis.

- Set phone alarms that go off several times a day with words that represent the qualities I'm being when I'm at my highest or how I desire to serve.
- Pray, or ask someone to pray for me.
- Take consistent action to create more of what I would rather see.
- Do something intentionally that gets me outside my comfort zone.
- Face my fear head on as much as possible.
- Ask for help when I need it, or when I get stuck.
- Keep a gratitude journal.
- Spend time in nature.
- Work out and exercise.
- Give thanks for a positive outcome in advance, especially when I'm scared.
- Listen to positive and uplifting music, especially when I'm in the soup bowl of life.

The more I implement the above faith building practices, the better I feel and the better results I get. These practices knock off the shards of clay that dampen your spirit so that your light and genius shines through.

Pruning

Pruning is like weeding. It involves cutting out the same things, but there is one distinct difference. Sometimes, we set off on a course and discover new information; information that we did not have prior to acting. Information that we need to account for in our decision and eliminating process.

For example, I know people who, once they start feeling better and getting better results, grow cocky or arrogant, letting their success go to their heads. They may treat others differently by being less kind and generous. This type of attitude and behavior needs pruning.

Conversely, sometimes people reach an unprecedented level of success and face a terrifyingly new level of fear. They worry about losing all they have achieved and find themselves wondering when the other shoe will fall as they anticipate that something bad must follow.

When this happens, it's time to take out the pruning shears and get to work. Apply the same recommendations found above in the segment on weeding.

Being Patient

Despite our desire for instant gratification, it's time to get present to how life works and to incorporate this wisdom into our expectations. To do this, let's look at nature. Albert Einstein once said: "Look deep into nature and then you will understand everything better."

I say nature teaches us how to feel better and get better results.

Stop Worrying and Complaining

The sun doesn't whine and complain because rain falls from the clouds. The moon doesn't complain that the sun is shining too much. A wolf doesn't moan in despair because it's not a moose. The tree sapling doesn't complain that it's too hard to grow into the mighty oak and give up trying.

A Season for Everything

Nature also demonstrates that there is a season for everything. Natural things occur in cycles, and there is an ebb and flow to life. When you plant a rose seed, there is a period where a lot is happening under the surface that we cannot see. Just because we cannot see the transformation the seed is undergoing, it does not mean nothing is happening. Yet, when we plant the seed of our dream or attempt to change something in our lives, many of us give up way too early because we do not see instant progress or change.

There is a Rhythm to Life

We also forget that there is a rhythm to life. Assuming we are fertile soil, we undergo seasons in the growth process of feeling better and realizing our dreams. The seed undergoes periods of transformation. It grows from a:

- Seed.
- Seedling with roots, a stem, leaves, and buds.
- Buds continue to grow and mature producing flowers.
- Flowers are pollinated turning into fruit.
- Fruits contain new seeds inside and ripen.
- Ripened fruit drops to the ground.
- Cycle begins again.

The seed does not agonize that it won't become a fruit and bear new seeds. It is what it is and navigates the stages of its growth with grace. Of course, the plant requires pollinators (e.g., bees, moths, butterflies, insects, and the wind) for the cycle to continue. Otherwise, the cycle is interrupted and the plant perishes.

We are like the seed. Our roots and stems need to establish before we can blossom into the bud. We need to grow and mature to blossom into the flower. We need positive and supportive people to pollinate us so that we bear the fruit of our dreams. As one dream manifests, it gives rise to the seeds of a new dream or desire, and the cycle begins again.

Faith makes us feel better. When we act with the conviction of our faith, we get better results. Faith is patient because when we are faith-filled, we trust the process. We trust that we are in the process of becoming that which we long to be and of having that which we long to manifest.

Trust the Process

Several years ago, I was driving on a narrow two-lane road when I noticed an oncoming car veering into my lane. There was nowhere for me to navigate to avoid a collision.

Next, the most incredible and strange thing happened, it felt as though a Loving Presence took over the wheel of my car.

I felt my car shift. No dramatic moves. Just a shift.

For a few seconds, it felt as if my car was flying as smoothly as an airplane at cruising altitude. After a few moments, things returned to normal. I cannot explain what happened, yet I am immensely grateful to have avoided what was sure to have been a horrible accident.

I love this story because I have no way of explaining what happened on the road that day to help me avoid being horribly injured in an automobile accident. Indeed, this story has a much better ending than other times in my life, where I've attempted to control the outcome by hanging onto the wheel tightly, attempting to force or make things into what I thought they should be.

I've learned that the more I attempt to force or control things, the more I squeeze the life energy right out of them. My need to control is greatest when I cave into fear. Whenever I cave into fear, pain overtakes me and the happiness, health, and fulfillment I desire eludes me.

Acting out of fear puts me in the same boat as someone who attempts to hang onto water by squeezing it. On the other hand, as I surrender to what love would have me do, and trust the process, I feel better and experience better results.

Surrender seems counterintuitive because we equate it with giving up, quitting, and losing. Surrender does *not* mean this. It is a process of letting go by releasing my gripping need to *control* things.

When I trust the process, I am confident that my dreams will result in a positive outcome, even though things may look quite different from what I had imagined. Surrender has me curious about many outcomes: What good and wonderful thing will happen because of this situation?

On the other hand, control has me resisting what is taking place and grumbling, "Why did this happen to me?"

Surrender does not imply submission to anyone or anything, nor does it ask me to forego my dreams and aspirations because people do not believe they are within reach. It doesn't mean that I give up on my dreams because someone disagrees with the path I take in pursuing them.

Think of surrender as choosing to release your need to control and entrusting the unfolding of your dreams to the Great Ocean, or Creative Flow, of life. When I use the word "surrender", I mean it in the context of the Irish Fisherman metaphor as told by Eileen Flanagan: "There is nothing wrong with swimming when we go overboard or in throwing a drowning man a rope, though trying to control the sea is as good a way to drown as is doing nothing at all."

Surrender means I accept that I am participating in the Something Greater happening all around me, that *is* me and that flows *through* me. I give up my need to cling to my identity and submit to the possibility that my Highest Self is continually showing up anew.

I let go of who I am in the moment to become who I am in the next moment so that I may realize my full potential.

As I release my gripping need to control things, and trust that my dreams—or something even better—will come to pass, I create the space necessary for creative magic to unfold. As I quiet the conversation in my mind and tune into that still, small voice within me, I am quietly nudged to explore avenues that I would not have considered pursuing before.

As I hop in the ocean of life, swimming, paddling, and doing whatever I can on my own behalf without needing to control, I create space for life's magic to wow and amaze me.

The following story is based on how life's magic wowed me one night when I was a firefighter.

Call It God, Call It Buddha, Call It Allah, Call It Intuition - An Arsonist Tale

As the first female firefighter for my county, I felt enormous pressure to prove myself to the guys and to prove to the world that women had a place in the fire service. I felt intense pressure to perform well and to exceed everyone's expectations in the hopes that 1), I would save lives, 2), the guys would accept me, and 3), I would make it easier for the women who entered the fire service behind me.

To achieve this, I relied heavily on my faith and intuition. What follows is a story of how faith and intuition saved my life on one call:

One crisp October night, around 12:30AM, the alarm sounded. The 9-1-1 operator signaled us to respond to a nearby structure fire. Arriving on the scene, we saw flames and smoke rolling out of the roof and the windows of the structure. The rickety old house looked abandoned, but we didn't know if a vagrant or anyone else was trapped inside. We did know that the fire had a substantial head start on us and that we did not want the structure to collapse on us—or anyone else potentially trapped inside the building.

I was assigned the role of nozzle man (my job was to spray water on the fire to extinguish the flames while my partner fed me the heavy, water-laden hoses). This kind of teamwork allowed us to maneuver quickly aroundobstacles like furniture that we encounter in such structures to get water on the flames as quickly as possible.

Time was of the essence.

As we entered the house, I fought back the flames as my partner worked behind me, feeding me more hose. The smoke was so thick I could barely see my hand in front of my face.

As I made a beeline directly toward the origin of the fire, something strange and otherworldly happened.

Suddenly, inexplicably, it felt as if someone—a magnetic force, not hands—grabbed my legs. The force was so strong, I couldn't move. My head was saying, "Go, go, go," but my body would not respond. The fire was growing stronger, the heat more intense, and the smoke ever thicker.

I couldn't move.

My partner yelled at me to get a move on in some rather colorful language designed to motivate me to get into action and do my job.

After what seemed like an eternity, even though it was only a few seconds, I managed to shout back to my partner, "Wait a minute; something's wrong!"

As suddenly as I'd been stopped dead in my tracks, I knew.

I intuitively knew that we had to progress toward the origin of the fire from a different direction than the one we took on our initial approach. I knew what path to take. I yelled this back at my partner who wasn't particularly amused with me, promptly instructing me to get my ass in gear, adding "I don't care how we do it—just do it!"

Once I intuitively knew the direction to proceed in, the magnetic force that held me in its grip set me free and in motion. Finding no one trapped inside, we worked our way around to the origin of the fire and extinguished the flames well before the building caved in on us.

Later, after the smoke cleared and after much teasing and general harassment from my fellow firefighters, we discovered that an arsonist had booby trapped the floor of the house.

Had we entered the structure and continued to advance toward the fire's origin as our training dictated, we would have fallen through the floor and into the trap below.

The arsonist's trap was designed to maim and kill. Had that invisible force not intervened, both my partner and I would have been injured and disfigured—if not killed.

I share this story to demonstrate, first and foremost, that things sometimes happen that we cannot explain. I can no more tell you what stopped me in my tracks on that day now than I could when it happened.

I also share it because even though I already believed in a Higher Power, call it God, call it Buddha, call it Allah, call it Spirit, call it Love, call it Tree, that experience heightened my awareness.

Through it, I learned to pay attention to and trust in the great invisible unknown far more than ever before I responded to that call. This experience also taught me the power of my intuition.

My almost-deadly encounter with the arsonist's trap also taught me that I may not see a way, but as I take a leap into the vast unknown, many things will conspire to help me on my quest. Action calls unforeseen coincidences forth that otherwise remain hidden when I sit on the sidelines of life in fear and disbelief.

Trusting the process means surrendering my need to control things. Fear pushes me to control myself, other people, and circumstances. Trust frees me from the murky fears that enslave me. As I trust the process, the shards of clay and muck that hold me back get knocked off. The more my stuff gets knocked off, the better I feel and the better results I get.

In meditation one morning, the following image came to me:

Imagine I'm an eagle, born equipped to soar.

Each time I buy into fear, one of my wings gets clipped.

I can fly with one or two wings clipped, but each wing that gets clipped hinders how high I'm able to fly.

Each time I let fear win over love, a wing gets clipped;

Each time I buy into "ain't it awful," a wing gets clipped;

Each time I buy into not enough, another wing gets clipped;

Each time I buy into the notion that things will never change, a wing gets clipped;

Wing after wing gets clipped until I can no longer fly.

Now I'm a grounded eagle, frustrated because I know I was born to fly.

Before I clipped my wings, I flew high above the clouds where the sun or Light is present even when it's rainy and stormy below.

My eagle spirit knows flight is my true nature.

But I'm stuck on the ground with my eagle wings clipped because I failed to manage the conversation in my eagle head and the conversations I have participated in with the people around me.

I'm cranky, irritable, angry, frustrated, hurt, wounded, sad, depressed, disappointed, fearful, and full of despair which keeps me stuck and grounded.

That is, until I develop the courage to start stretching my wings in new, uncharted directions—by changing the conversations I have with myself and others.

Surrendering creates the space necessary for me to learn, grow, and mature. Trusting the process equips me with eagle wings so that I can excel and soar in life. The more I trust the process, the more time I spend on the balcony and out of the soup bowl of life.

What would make you feel better?

- Is there something you want to see changed in your life or in the world?
- Make a list of five to seven things that are important to you that you would like to be different. Apply the formula. Without faith, you already know the results.

- Allow yourself, for one moment, to believe that the change you want to see is possible as you step out in faith trusting your inner inspiration more than your outer sensations. What actions are you inspired to take now?

- What faith-filled steps will you take when you encounter obstacles along the way?

- What strategies will you implement to stretch your imagination?

- How will you train yourself to rely on your inner vision to avoid getting bogged down by what you can't or don't see yet?

- List your accomplishments. What contributed to your success?

- How will you leverage this to create what you want to see more of in your world?

- Is there any area in your life where you lack faith? Who has been successful in that area? What can you learn from them to strengthen your faith?

- In the areas where your faith is strong, how might you leverage your faith to help someone who is struggling?

- What courageously faith-filled actions will you take each day?

- How will you cultivate yourself so that the seeds of your dreams flourish?

- What strategies and methods will you use to keep your vision of you at your highest and best in your awareness?

- What tools will you implement to keep the seeds of your vision in front of you?

- What weeds do you need to remove?

- What tools will you use to water and fertilize yourself and the seeds of your vision?

- What needs pruning?

- How can you be more patient?

- Are you willing to surrender and trust the process?

- Are you willing to change the conversation you are and the conversation you have with others in favor of feeling better and getting better results?
- What do you need to let go of so that life works for you and the people around you?
- How good are you at listening to your intuition?
- Have you left enough wiggle room for the magic of the universe to wow you—or do you continue to attempt to control everything?

Chapter 7

The Seventh Courageous Practice – Getting Tight with God

The seventh courageous practice that reduces our pain also helps us feel better and get better results. I call it getting tight with God (or whatever name you call your Creator).

As a reminder, I am not a religious person; I am a spiritual person. While this chapter is about God, it is not written from the point of view of any religion. Rather, it is a practice that anyone, regardless of their spiritual or religious affiliations, can practice.

Question: What is the one constant in a relentlessly changing world?

Answer: Creation

Throughout history and around me right now, new things are continuously being created. The fact that new things are constantly being created fascinates me, given the penchant human beings have for resisting change.

Imagine what your life would be like without the mop, the kitchen stove, a flush toilet, clothes hangers, a dishwasher, a motorized vacuum cleaner, the refrigerator, paper towels, an ATM, automated teller machine, and conversations.

To connect with the flow of life powerfully, it's imperative for me to dance with the ever-changing process of Creation. I call this ever-unfolding process of Creation "God". The more connected I feel to the Creation Process—or God—the better I feel.

God

As with other words, the word God evokes whole worlds of meanings and images for people. When I use the word car, the image that pops into your mind is probably different than the image of a car that pops up in my mind. The same is true for the word God. What comes up for you when you hear the word God?

- Is it an image, a feeling, or perhaps nothing at all?
- Is God an entity you turn to in times of trouble, or do you talk with God like a trusted friend every day?
- Where are you at when you feel most connected to God (e.g., church, synagogue, temple, mosque, in nature, on the football field, at home)?
- What are you doing when you feel most connected to God (e.g., meditating, praying, playing certain music, singing, cooking, or playing your favorite sport)?
- How does the idea of God make you feel (e.g., fearful, ambivalent, comforted)?
- Do you trust that God is looking out for your best interests, or does it seem like God has too many things that are way more important than you?
- How close do you feel to God on a daily basis (e.g., not close at all, somewhat distant, sometimes close/sometimes distant, close, or exceptionally close)?

What if I told you your experiences in life, good and bad, are directly correlated to how you view God?

When you don't like how things are going in your life, what if all you need to do to turn things around is to get a better idea of God?

What if your ability to feel better and achieve better results is connected to what you believe about God?

I say this rings true.

It rings true for most people because what we believe about God influences the relationship we have with the Creation Process. It rings true because how well we dance with the Creative Process impacts how much pain we are in, how we heal—or don't, and how we treat other people.

Notice I asked you *what if?*

While I think I'm on to something when I observe how the quality of a person's state of being is connected to what that person believes about God and how they relate to God, I do not claim to have the God's Eye View. I am one person with one point of view attempting to describe something far greater than the elephant the blind men were attempting to describe earlier in the book.

I mindfully asked you *what if* because I'm extending an invitation for you to consider something that may improve the quality of your life, should you choose to accept the invitation.

Whether you realize it or not, you and I were born into, and/or subscribe to a God paradigm. This God paradigm influences how you and I dance with each other, how we relate to other people, and how we dance with life. Our God paradigms are full of ideas about how things should be done, made, and thought about.

God paradigms also establish rules and boundaries and provide guidance on how to solve problems that exist inside those boundaries. In short, these paradigms are models or systems designed to solve problems.

Your God paradigm impacts your ability to enjoy yourself and get the best out of life. Religion has merit, but most religions are closed and inflexible, limiting people to following that specific religion's doctrine, rules, and practices. They require people to believe and do things their way—or face dire consequences (e.g., not fitting in, not belonging, making people outside their religion bad and wrong, and/or condemning people to hell).

For me, approaching God and the world this way is limiting.

This approach, or paradigm of God, is too narrow, too confining, and fails to accurately account for the abundance that naturally exists in the universe. For instance, God, the Creator of the entire Universe is so abundant that God created approximately:

- 400,000 species of flowering plants.
- 10,000,000 colors the human eye can see.
- 950,000 species of insects.
- 100,000 tree species.
- 6,909 languages spoken throughout the world.
- 5,416 mammal species.
- 1,500 musical instruments.
- 340 dog breeds.
- 30 words for snow in Eskimo.
- 7.4 billion people in the world, with only one of you and only one of me.

When I observe such naturally occurring abundance in the world, it's clear to me that God has far more pathways to accomplish things than my human individual can possibly imagine.

The problem with God paradigms is that they act like filters that screen all the available information that comes into our minds. Information that agrees with our God paradigm passes through our filters easily, but any inputs that do *not* fit our God paradigm are very difficult for us to see. The more exceptional the data is, the more our filters interfere with our ability to see.

Human beings select input that fits best with their rules and attempt to ignore the rest. In a sense, our paradigms physiologically render us incapable of perceiving data that does not fit our paradigm. The screening effect of paradigms makes exceptional data invisible, and makes us blind.

What follows are several concepts of God given to us by various religious traditions. In each description offered, imagine how you would relate to your Creator and to life if that particular model of God were the only accurate one. If you discover one of the concepts offered below matches your own paradigm about God, explore these questions:

- How does this concept serve me (i.e., make my life better, make me a better human being)?
- What does this concept tell me about who I am and what I'm capable of?
- How does this concept limit me (i.e., make me fearful, remembering that the opposite of love is fear)?
- Does this concept limit how God can show up for me? If so, how?

God as Nature and Spirits

Some cultures believe God exists in every plant, tree, animal, and rock, grain of sand particle of dirt, river, lake, and stream. Some cultures believe that the world is inhabited by invisible spirits (sometimes called angels) who mysteriously appear to guide or help us mere humans. Traditions such as these are most closely linked to Paganism, Shamanism, Gnosticism, andthe teachings of Native American tribes.

Old Man in the Sky God

Many people have an image of God as a wise, old, white-bearded man located somewhere in the sky above the clouds looking down on his creation. They experience God as distant and removed from them. The Old Man in the Sky God arbitrarily rains down his favor and blessings on his creations—or punishment to those who go astray. Traditions such as these are most closely linked to some denominations of Christianity.

Scorekeeper God

Scorekeeper God is similar to the Old Man in the Sky God in that he, too, is distant and removed from his creations. Unlike the arbitrary manner in which the Old Man in the Sky God doles out favor and punishment, Scorekeeper God has a Big Book and keeps track of each sin, mistake, and depraved act you've ever committed in your life to determine what your fate will be after you die and meet him on the day of reckoning. He decides whether you make it into heaven…or go to hell. Traditions such as these are most closely linked to some denominations of Christianity and Islam.

Impersonal Lawful God

Some religious teachings speak of God as an Impersonal Higher Power that impartially applies universal spiritual laws to and/or on behalf of Its creations. This God is sometimes depicted as a Divine Cosmic Cocktail Waitress or Sugar Daddy God who always says, "Yes," to our requests. For example, if a person says, "I get the best breaks," God says, "Yes," and it seems like good opportunities often come their way. By the same token if a person says, "Nothing ever works out for me," God says, "Yes," and nothing ever seems to work out for that person. Traditions such as these are most closely linked to some nondenominational Christian teachings, New Age, and Metaphysical teachings.

There Is No God

Referred to as atheists, some people do not believe God or gods exist, or they lack belief in the existence of any deities.

Container-less God

Some spiritual traditions do not claim the existence of any one God or prophet, nor do they worship any one God, nor do they believe in any one philosophic concept. Traditions like these do not address or concern themselves with the origin of the world. These teachings, or ways of life, do not satisfy the traditional features of a religion. Rather, they are focused on methods for improving the quality of a person's life. Traditions such as these are most closely linked to Buddhism, Hinduism, and Confucianism.

God Is All There Is

Other religious customs teach that God Is All There Is and that every animate and inanimate object is an expression or extension of God. Everything is comprised of God Substance. There is no separation between objects and God; all objects, including human beings, are one with God. Traditions such as these are most closely linked to quantum theories and spiritual philosophies found in New Age and Metaphysical teachings.

These are but a few models people use to describe their God paradigm. Which one is the most accurate? I don't think it matters. What is more important is understanding how your God paradigm impacts your ability to feel good, get the results you want and enjoy life. What matters more is:

- Does your concept of God improve or detract from your quality of life?
- Does your concept of God empower you to be your best?
- Does your concept of God empower you to treat other people with respect, compassion, and leave them with their dignity intact and whole?
- Does your God paradigm have you feeling optimistic and hopeful about your future and the afterlife?

If your answers to the above questions demonstrate that your God paradigm has a favorable influence on you and each aspect of your life is working for you, great! Keep on keeping on. However, your God paradigm may not be working well for you if it:

- Interferes with your ability to enjoy life while not harming or placing limits on others.
- Leaves you feeling inferior or disconnected from God, life's possibilities, and other people.

- Keeps you stuck in judging/voting, right/wrong, good/bad conversations.
- Makes you feel superior to other people.
- Makes you ultra-critical of people who appear to be different than you.
- Makes you critical of people whose concept of God is different than your own.
- Requires you to give up on your dreams because some sacred text or religious authority figure tells you that you must do so.

Whether you are religious or spiritual, Creation ebbs and flows. The farmer plants the seed, waters the seeds and fertilizes them before they turn into crops bearing fruit. The rose blossoms, the rose petals fall away and decay before the birth of the new buds begin.

The difference between the farmer's crop, the rose, and me is that they are not slaves to whatever form they appear in moment-to-moment (i.e., they are not attached to their identity). The farmer's crop and the rose do not fight the changes that occur throughout their lifecycle. With beauty, they evolve gracefully as they make the transition from birth to life to death as the process echoes itself repeatedly through the eons.

As God blesses the farmer's crop and the rose with the beauty and grace needed to move through the changes in their lives, God blesses you and me with the grace we need to move beautifully through the changes in our lives.

Sometimes I face situations that do not appear to have a logical solution. No matter how much I attempt to map out how I am going to get from where I am to where I want to be, I cannot see how to make it happen.

When I don't know how to make something happen, it would be easy for me to say it can't be done. I may declare this is just the way the world is. Once I declare that it can't be done, I give up on it ever happening.

When I don't see how to do something that matters to me, I've learned that I am better served by turning my mind off and by stopping my attempts to figure it out.

When I don't see a way, it's time for me to stop overanalyzing, and it's time for me to stop surfing the internet in search of a solution. When I don't know how, it's time for me to stop leaning on my own understanding and to choose to lean on and trust in God.

Choosing to lean on and trust in God requires me to trust that God will bring about a favorable solution. It also requires me to listen differently. I need to quiet my mind so I hear that still small voice within me. This involves more of a sensory experience than knowledge-seeking or a physical hands-on kind of experience.

There is a difference in an experiential or sensory understanding of something and knowing about something. For instance, take the word *wind*. There is a distinct difference between learning the definition of wind: the movement of air, and having the experience of feeling the wind blowing on your face.

There is a difference between knowing the definition of wind and using wind to fill up the sails of your boat in a way that moves your boat forward.

There is also a difference between receiving instructions on how to do something and the actual sensory experience of doing it as illustrated in the following description of how to ride a bike.

1. Stand over the top tube of the bicycle with both feet planted on the ground.

2. While keeping one foot on the ground, place the other foot on a pedal raised to the 2 o'clock position (front pedal).

3. Press down on the on the front pedal while placing your other foot on the other bike pedal.

4. While balancing your body on the bike's two wheels, alternate pressing down on each pedal to propel yourself forward.

The instructional description of how to ride a bike is different from the physical and sensory experience of riding a bike. This is true for many things in life. Knowing about something does not necessarily mean we have had direct experience of it.

The Artistry of Life

Consider this: we can describe the techniques the painter uses to create a masterpiece, but the vision for the painting comes from an invisible space inside the painter.

Music provides another example. A person can learn how to play an instrument, but the music comes from an invisible place within them. The rhythm, the beat, and the lyrics are inside the player of the music, not the instrument itself.

How did the painting or the music get inside of the artist in the first place?

God.

Right now, you may be thinking "OK, but I'm not an artist or musician!" What if you are both the artist and the instrument? What if you are God's instrument and the two of you together create the music and artwork that's called your life?

The creative spark of genius lies within the Invisible you that exists far above and beyond your physical body and your external circumstances. You are actively involved in a co-Creative Process, moment-by-moment, as you make the decisions and choices you make throughout each day.

You are automatically absorbed in the Creative Process with every breath you take and with each thought you have. The key to enjoying an extraordinary life lies within your ability to put more stock in the Invisible Power of God to make your hearts desires manifest than you do in what is visible to you now.

In the end, when all is said and done, we are in this thing called life together. We are part of something greater that's taking place. We each see one tiny part of the Giant, Vast Whole. We have more in common than external appearances make things seem.

We are born and we will die. In between birth and death, every soul longs to be free from pain and suffering, to feel their best, and to get the best results possible.

What will make you feel better?

- How can you align yourself better with the Creation Process?
- What steps will you take to learn to dance with the ever-changing process of Creation more effectively?
- What comes up for you when you hear the word, God?
- How do you view God?
- Does your definition and/or model of God enhance your life and your sense of well-being? If not, what do you need to adjust to make it work better?
- Is your God paradigm serving you well, or, does it need expansion?
- Have you had a direct experience of God versus a theoretical, intellectual experience?
- If you've had a direct experience of God, how can you leverage what you experienced to your advantage?
- If have not had a direct experience, what steps are you willing to take to have one? (Hint: Having an experience of something requires us to do something, usually something outside our comfort zone).
- If you are the instrument, what music are you playing? What music do you long to play?
- If you are the artist, what are you painting? What art do you long to paint?
- How will you practice putting more stock in God so more magic can happen?
- How might you improve your relationship with God?

Chapter 8

The Eighth Courageous
Practice – It Takes a Village

The eighth courageous practice is about building and nurturing community. It takes a village to see the whole elephant and to make sense of this extraordinary thing called life, as we each see and experience one part of a greater whole.

Taking pictures on vacation, I've been surprised from time to time to discover a person cluttering up what I considered my perfect shot. Some people purposefully photobomb unsuspecting photographers, but sometimes we can be so focused on one thing that we lose sight of everything else around us. In firefighting, we call this tunnel vision.

We all get tunnel vision when it comes to our perspective. Perspective includes:

- Judgments.
- Beliefs.
- What we are being right about.
- Our communication.
- Drama.
- What upsets us.
- How we interpret what we see.

My perspective on people, life and death changed significantly when I became a firefighter. My views were further altered from being my county's first female firefighter. The same is true for you. Your life experiences shape your perspective.

The problem is sometimes our perception is not accurate. Remember the story about the air conditioning not working in my van? That story was harmless. Sometimes the cost of our faulty perception can be devastating.

I heard a story once about a young woman who wanted her grandmother's pearl necklace upon her grandmother's death. The young woman's mother promised her that she would give them to her at the appointed time. The grandmother passed, and the daughter came home for a visit expecting to receive her grandmother's necklace.

After dinner, with sparkling eyes, her mother pointed to a chest. It was the grandmother's hope chest. She told the young woman that her grandmother wanted her to have that chest.

Disappointed, the young woman stomped out of her parents' home and never spoke to her mother again. When the mother died, the young woman returned home. Going through her mother's things, she saw her grandmother's hope chest.

Rummaging through it, she discovered many items; a handmade quilt, silver napkin holders, a savings bond, some cash, and a velvet jewelry box. Inside the jewelry box, she found her grandmother's pearl necklace with a note from her mother.

The mother had written how proud she was of her daughter, and about how much she loved her. The mother explained that she wanted her daughter to start out with far more than what she started out with as a young woman going out into the world on her own.

In the story, the young woman had tunnel vision. She was looking to receive a pearl necklace, not a hope chest. She was upset. The daughter was convinced that her mother had not given her what she wanted. From her perspective, her mother had really let her down.

She severed her relationship with her mother because her tunnel vision had her convinced she was right. All the while, the daughter had access to the greater good she was seeking (e.g., the necklace).

Yet because it did not come in the package the daughter expected, she could not see it. All that the young woman needed to do to receive her greater good was unwrap the package she was given.

Tunnel vision limits my perspective and may cause me to miss the gift contained inside the packages (e.g., people, opportunities, jobs, joy) right in front of my eyes. It takes a village to see what I, alone, cannot see.

Imagine how differently things could have turned out if someone had encouraged the young woman to address her upset with her mom.

Imagine what might have happened had someone encouraged her to go back to her parents' home and open the hope chest the next day.

It takes a village to see what I cannot see. It takes a village to open me up to new, more empowering, possibilities.

We tend to think that our happiness increases or decreases based on external factors.

Someone cuts me off in traffic and I feel angry.

I got laid off from my job and that makes me sad.

I scored the winning goal for my team so I'm elated.

The doctor gave me my test results and I feel relieved.

I got a raise at work and that makes me happy.

In short, something happens called an event, and I feel something about the event. Events happen and we feel happy, sad, mad, glad, angry, or disappointed based on those events.

The problem with this approach is that it leaves us at the mercy of the circumstances we are in while keeping our experience of happiness fleeting and elusive. This approach suggests that we have littletono control over how happy or unhappy we are.

Stuff happens, right?

This outlook fails to recognize that there is a gap between the event and how I feel. What if it goes like this:

- An event happens.
- I have a thought about the event, usually a judgment about it being good/bad.
- Depending on what I told myself about the event, I have a feeling about it (scared, angry, sad, depressed, excited, elated, or happy).

When viewed this way, events are not good or bad as the Farmer Story illustrated in Stuff 101. Events are things that happen based on facts which are measurable. I am the one who gives meaning to an event by the story I tell about it.

The world is full of people participating in the drama story. Our decision to participate in the drama, or step off the drama dance floor, influences how we feel. How we feel moves us to act or to remain inactive. Victim choices lead to more victimization. Placing positive, affirmative and empowering thoughts in the gap leads to inspired action with triumphant outcomes.

Imagine being in a community that encourages you to expand your vision and stop playing victim. Imagine being in a community that supports you in achieving the results you desire by coaching you to place thoughts in the gap that are in alignment with the results you wish to achieve. It takes a village.

The story about the young woman and the pearl necklace illustrated how unfulfilled expectations generate upsets that have a significant impact on relationships.

Expectations are formulated from:

- A promise or agreement between myself and another person.
- What I've experienced in previous relationships.
- What I saw growing up.
- My fears (i.e., of being abandoned, of not measuring up, of being unworthy).
- Generalizations about groups of people (e.g., men/women always, leaders are a certain way, religious people are a certain way).

My expectations are the impetus that drives me to act. How I react is based on what I place into the gap, or what I make up about the other person's behavior. This is where it gets interesting. Every time there is a discrepancy between my expectations and the other person's behavior, I have a choice.

I can choose to believe the best—or I can choose to assume the worst.

I choose what I put in the gap every single time something happens. My judgments, thoughts, and beliefs create the life I'm living today. Creating a happy marriage or a happy life requires me to make one consistent choice, and that is to choose to believe the best. The more proficient I am at believing the best, the better I feel and the better results I get.

Imagine being part of a community that lovingly addresses expectations and the upsets that occur when there is a breakdown. Imagine how empowering it will be to stand among villagers who believe the best about you and about the thing you want to create. Imagine them believing in your possibilities and supporting you as you set out to create that which you dream about. Imagine the members of your community championing you to be your best, as you cheer them on to be their best. It takes a village.

Most people agree that firefighters, police officers, and coast guard rescue workers are courageous. Courage means feeling the fear and doing it anyway. All it takes to be brave is to love someone so much that you are willing to risk your life for them or to want something so much that you are willing to risk looking foolish to achieve it. You are courageous!

Imagine being part of a community that gives your courage wings so you can fly.

Firefighters are taught to thoroughly examine everything around the burning structure before rushing in to put the fire out. That means making a quick check of the entire perimeter before heading in to make the rescue and/or extinguish the fire. This practice is called surveying the scene.

As you survey the scene or the world around you in pursuit of your dream, it's common to experience periods of doubt and fear. Creating something that we've never created before involves risk. For many people, taking risks is a scary proposition. In life, playing for your dreams requires risk and uncertainty.

To become the thing I want to become, I must let go of the current image I have of myself. To achieve the thing I want to achieve, I must leave the familiar behind and travel into unchartered territory. There will be people who think I'm foolish. They may call me unflattering names. They may ridicule me. I might not succeed in the grand way I envision. Like Martin Luther King, Jr., I might not fully realize my dream in my lifetime.

All of those are risks that I face.

Spotting a risk shouldn't stop me from pursuing that which I love and care about. When firefighters spot a hidden danger surveying a scene, they don't immediately give up because the odds appear insurmountable. Instead, they look for a way to work around the challenge, the risks, and the danger, and then they work together to overcome them.

Imagine being part of a community that supports you in overcoming your doubts and fears as you pursue what you love and care about. It takes a village.

Your commitment to your dream is one of your greatest assets. Commitment bridges the gap between your fears and the realization of your dreams. Commitment transports you to create what you love and care about. Without commitment, dreams crash and burn.

When one is committed, miracles unfold.

Commitment is about closing the back door and closing our escape hatch. I can tell I'm not fully committed when I place conditions on my level of participation in pursuing my goal. For example, I may say things like:

- Once I have $500,000 saved for start-up money, I'll pursue my dream of starting my own business.
- I'll exercise four times a week if I can find the time.
- If people constantly praise me, I'll pursue my dream to dance.
- I'll open my own coffee shop if my friends agree that it's a good idea.

Whenever I place a condition on my dream or goal, I'm not fully committed. Being committed means I commit to playing full out for the thing I aspire to no matter what.

It means I don't let circumstances dictate my future. I take full responsibility for the results I get. I continue to learn, grow, and develop myself until I achieve the thing I set out to achieve.

I don't blame anyone for keeping me from my goal. Instead, I find a way to go around obstacles, over them, under them, or through them— or a different way altogether to accomplish my dream.

Imagine being in a community that points out how fear gets in your way, cheers you on despite your doubts, and respectfully holds you accountable for the commitments you make to yourself. It takes a village to create this kind of magical space.

Based on my understanding of commitment, I discovered that I'm not committed to all that much. There are not that many things I love and care about so much so that I'm willing to die in pursuit of doing or having.

Having fewer commitments gives me more energy, focus, and time to devote to the things I am committed to doing and having. This allows me to gain more traction and make more progress in the areas of my life that matter to me most. By concentrating my energy this way, I have a greater impact on the things that I love and care about the most.

Imagine having more energy, focus, and time to devote yourself to the things you are committed to doing and having. Imagine the traction you would gain and the progress you would make in the areas of your life that are most important to you. Imagine your fellow villagers supporting you in your commitments to be and/or do what matters most to you. It takes a village.

You have what it takes to do what you love and to become the kind of person you wish to become.

It can feel daunting to step outside your comfort zone in pursuit of your dreams. You may worry about people making fun of you, disappointing your loved ones, failure, money, and thousands of other things. Even when you muster up the courage to take those first steps towardyour dream, you may encounter resistance from people who don't want you to change.

Imagine what a difference it would make to have other people pulling for you, encouraging you and speaking words of favor into you when you step outside of your comfort zone. It takes a village.

The number one deterrent that keeps your dreams from coming true is fear.

When you let fear get in your way, you stop pursuing that which you love and care for. When this happens, everyone loses.

Imagine being surrounded by villagers who understand:

- *Their stuff.*
- *Your stuff.*
- *How fear steals our joy.*
- *How to conquer fear and live a triumphant life.*
- *How to support you in being your best.*

A community like this can keep us on track and create phenomenal results in our world. It takes a village.

To feel our best and get the best results possible requires community. It takes a village to raise a child, and it takes community to bring out our best. I would not have succeeded as a firefighter without my fellow firefighters. Any Olympic athlete, gifted musical composer, talented CEO, or successful parent knows there is no substitution for being in a community of people who believe in you and expect more from you.

I have a vision of who I am when I am operating at my highest and best. I have an image of what I'm doing when I am at my highest and best. By now, you do too. My vision involves creating a world that works for everyone.

I cannot realize this dream without a village or community.

You can't realize your dreams without community.

I need people in my community who understand their stuff, how their fear robs them of joy, kills relationships, and the various ways our fear causes our pain. I need people in my village who call me on my stuff and who hold me accountable for being my best, and you do too.

I'm scared about this because I have experienced the sting that sometimes comes with being held accountable. I appreciate that sometimes I am so afraid that I'd rather roll over, go belly up and play/stay small.

You've probably felt this way before too. Even so, I'm clear that I am capable of far more than I give myself credit for, and you are too.

When you look at your life, at what's working and at what's not working, you can appreciate that it takes a village to make things work. Villages that bring out the best in us open the door to us manifesting things greater than we are capable of manifesting on our own. Villagers committed to feeling their best and striving to get the best results have a way of upping our game.

They show us the areas we need to polish to knock off more shards of pain. They also highlight and strengthen our natural talents. Like the blind men and the elephant, our fellow villagers afford us a glimpse at the Big Picture that we do not have access to on our own.

I've experienced community as a powerful means to knocking off the shards of painand fear that hide the Light within me. I benefit from having trusted others remind me to shift my conversation away from fear and limiting ideas toward more expansive and empowering ideas.

My fellow villagers support me by offering me more expansive and/or empowering possibilities when I bump up against fear and/or a limiting idea. For example:

Limiting Idea	Expansive/Empowering Idea
Ain't it awful?	What's right/good about my life is <fill in the blank>.
Poor me.	This is an opportunity for me to <fill in the blank> (e.g., stand up for myself, ask for what I want, move on to something better).
What's wrong with people?	What works about people? What do the people in my life do well?
Yes, but <I'm afraid>.	This is an opportunity for me to learn and develop my faith muscles...to Trust in God's love.

| My feelings are hurt. | What's possible when I view this situation or person with trust and love? How will I interpret this in a more empoweringway? |
| I'm scared. | With God for me, all things are possible. I am protected. Something good will come from this situation. |

Though it might sting, I benefit from being held accountable for behaving in ways and engaging in activities that keep me stuck in the pain cycle. You benefit from being held accountable too.

I'm talking about a village filled with people who are more interested in my well-being than they are in being nice to me or validating my feelings. I am talking about a village filled with people who are more interested in my dreams coming true than they are in being right about anything.

I have benefited when the people in my village were kind and compassionate toward me while also loving me enough to call me on my stuff when I let my BS drama story get the better of me.

I've got further in life by having people who love me enough to encourage me to move forward when sneaky fear has got the best of me. It takes courage to be this kind of villager and to offer this kind of support.

You would benefit from having people compassionately call you on your stuff when you let your BS story get the best of you too. You would benefit from being supported in getting sneaky fear's hooks out of you too.

It takes a village of dedicated souls to realize humanity's potential. I benefit from villagers who they tell me when I'm off-track because sometimes I don't realize I'm off-track. Sometimes, you don't realize you are off-track. I benefit from engaging in conversations that are full of faith in positive outcomes. You do too.

Most of us do not experience community this way. Community appears to be full of discord, dissonance, and dissension. However, I say that it's possible to train myself to implement the eight courageous practices in this book to create the kind of village and villagers capable of creating a world that works.

If you are looking for a village full of visionary, faith-filled, huge hearted people, full of villagers who courageously implement the eight practices contained in this book, I invite you to join the conversation. To join the conversation, go to www.denisegarret.com.

In closing, let me remind you that you are meant to shine.

It is when we don't shine, or feel we are not acknowledged for our shininess, that our fear gets activated.

Our fear creates the dysfunction that occurs: the upsets, the mischief, the sickness, the violence, and the messiness. We also get upset when we've given someone a chance to shine and they fail.

We think that that we have to work hard at something in order for us to shine. This is a hidden paradigm that impacts our ability to realize our God given potential.

In reality, when we are living our life's purpose and doing what we love, we automatically shine. While effort is required, there is an easiness and a sense of spaciousness and expansiveness about it. When we live our life in service and do what we love, fuel gets pumped into our tank energizing us.

When we settle for less and buy into fear, we experience depletion. Fighting against our nature and the nature of others creates turbulence, violence, disrespect, distrust, and most of the other aches and pains in our livesresulting in humanity's suffering. It is not God doing this to us. It is not God who denies us. It is we who do it to ourselves and each other by not managing our fears and by failing to take responsibility for changing our limiting beliefs.

Remember the abundance in nature. God intends for us to shine, to thrive, and to prosper. It's time for us to get our shine on and to assist others in getting their shine on too.

I hope the tools and insights contained in this book have you feeling better and getting better results in your life.

I believe and declare that this book opens new possibilities for you to feel better and get better results.

I believe and declare that as you faithfully implement the eight courageous practices, you will shine like you've never shined before.

As you shift into playing full out in pursuit of your dreams, I offer you these final words of wisdom:

- Don't let fear get the best of you.
- Don't take yourself too seriously.
- Play for your dreams rather than your comfort.
- Let go of being right and choose what works.
- And, most importantly – Have Fun!

Become a member of the Eight Courageous Practices village now.

*To learn more about how to master the Eight Courageous Practices, go to:*www.denisegarrett.com.

A Special Bonus from Denise

Now that you have your copy of *Made to Thrive: Eight Courageous Practices to Improve Your Life, Find Inner Peace and Be Happy*, you are on your way to:

- Feeling better about yourself (i.e., who you are and how you interact with others)
- Feeling optimistic about your opportunities and possibilities
- Getting better results in your relationships, at work and at play

Plus...you'll soon find yourself experiencing more peace and happiness.

You'll also receive the special bonus journal I created to add to your toolkit. The journal gives you a central place to capture your responses to the questions contained inside. You may want to refer back to your answers as you grow and expand, or face different challenges moving forward.

There's so much confusing information out there about how to improve your life, find inner peace and happiness. When you finish this book, you'll be armed with eight courageous practices that will help you feel better and get better results.

While this journal is offered for sale, as a special bonus you can claim it for free here:

www.denisegarrett.com/bookbonus.

I believe you were made to thrive.

I'm in your corner. Let me know if I can help further.

Here's to you creating a life where you positively thrive!

Best,
Denise Garrett

Appendix

Belief Inventory

Belief Inventory	
1. Myself	23. Spirituality
2. My childhood	24. Health
3. My family	25. Weight
4. My parents	26. Fitness
5. My sibling(s)	27. What's right about me
6. My spouse	28. What's right about people
7. My children	29. What's right about the world
8. Work	30. What's wrong with me
9. Money	31. What's wrong with people
10. Prosperity	32. What's wrong with the world
11. Wealth	33. Success
12. Creative self-expression	34. Failure
13. Supply	35. What's feminine
14. Resources	36. What's masculine
15. Beauty	35. Love
16. Happiness	36. Hate
17. Peace	37. Violence
18. Joy	38. Crime
19. Play	39. Punishment
20. Fun	40. Power
21. God	41. Influence
22. Religion	42. What the world needs is:

About the Author

Denise Garrett appreciates the God-ness in people from all walks of lifeand is passionate about creating a world that works for everyone.

From growing up gay in a southern Baptist hometo becoming the first female firefighter in Gwinnett County, Georgia, and through serving in the role of counselor and personal development coach for over 20 years, Denise is living proof of how spiritual practices help people overcome obstacles to lead a richer, more fulfilling life.

Denise earned her Master of Social Work degree in 1996 from the University of Georgia. Denise has made major contributions in the areas of personal development coaching, mental and public health, emergency response, and disaster preparedness.

Considering herself a spiritual person versus a religious person, her personal philosophy is that God is too big to fit any one religion. Through her unique blend of no-nonsense compassion, her unique listening style, humor, story-telling, and deep love for God, she supports people in appreciating how remarkable and magnificent they are.

Go beyond the book and continue your journey with additional teachings from Denise Garrett that promote spiritual growth and well-being through courageous living practices.
Visit www.denisegarrett.com.

Made in the USA
Columbia, SC
17 November 2017